A Century in the North Peace
The Life and Times
of Anne and John Callison

Zat-So Productions
Montreal
2018

A Century in the North Peace
The Life and Times
of Anne and John Callison

by Erín Moure
with Anne Callison, North Peace Pioneer

ISBN: 978-0-9867595-2-9

Fifth Printing: March 2020, with minor corrections.

Zat-So Productions
Montréal, Québec, Canada
zatso.productions@gmail.com

Legal Deposit: Library and Archives Canada 2018 (First Printing)

Life is uncharted territory.
It reveals its story one moment at a time.

Leo Buscalgia
(words dear to Anne Callison)

this book is dedicated
to Anne's youngest grandchild, Isobel, and to all the grandchildren and
great-grandchildren, and to the generations to come

Anne and John heading from Old Fort Nelson to airport, 1940s

A Century in the North Peace
The Life and Times of Anne and John Callison
written and edited
by Erín Moure *for* Anne Callison, *Peace River Pioneer*

Introduction

the why of this book

This is, in a way, a family story. I am in it and involved in it, yet I am not at its centre. I did, however, eat its moosemeat. In fact, I grew up in part on the moosemeat of this story, which came to me as a child from my Aunt Anne and Uncle John Callison, via a long Greyhound bus ride from the North Peace District north of Fort St. John, down south to where Anne's sister, my mother Mary, lived in Calgary.

Today, fed by this moosemeat of childhood, I am but writer of this book, charged with a mission by Anne Callison, pioneer with her husband John in the North Peace River country. She is a woman whose life spans nearly a century, and bears witness to an important tale of early 20th century settlement in the area of Fort Nelson, Fort St. John, and Dawson Creek, places most non-Indigenous people know today as areas of big electrical power dams, reservoirs that drown valleys, of the fabled Alaska Highway, of pipelines and the booms and busts of oil and natural gas. Indigenous people view it differently, and this book acknowledges their experience too, although the fullness of their experience is something this book can only listen to, for their story is not mine to tell. But I need to make space for it.

Though the Callison family story is traversed by these vital events of the 20th century, events that marked the area forever, this is a different story, a small story, told in and beside those bigger stories.

It is the story of two people, Anne and John Callison, of how they grew, and how they came to be in this country of the North Peace River in British Columbia, in Canada, the traditional territory of the Dane-zaa (Beaver) people, overlapping and adjoining territories of Tsek'ene (Sekani) and other Athapaskan-speaking Dene peoples, also inhabited by westward migrations of Cree and Métis, many of whose families intertwined over time. It is the story of how Anne and John came into the world in other colonized lands, in North Dakota, USA, and in what is today western Ukraine, of how they came separately with their immigrating families to the lands of the Peace. It is the wonderful story of how they met, and came to spend 52 years of marriage together before John's death in 1996, and how they raised their family together, what conditions they lived under, what work they did as trappers, homesteading farmers, guides, freighters, hunters, hoteliers, and surveyors. It is an account of how they helped build communities and face the challenges and heartbreaks along the way, while history unfolded around them and changed their lives.

It is a story that could take place in no other century or place, and that, too, is part of its value.

Anne Callison is adventurous. She's spirited and feisty, has opinions and with a sideways humorous glance, always lets us know them. Even in 2018, at ninety-six, partly deprived of speech due to a stroke and living in an extended care home, her eyes light up with mischief and adventure when we talk about this book project we share.

There we have it: I am a ghost writer who is not a ghost. These words are mine and I am involved, but the stories come to me from members of the extended family of Callisons, from Anne and John's children, from my brother Bill who lived with Anne and John for two summers as a young teenager in the early 1970s, from my cousin Shona, daughter of Anne's brother Joe, and from me, daughter of Mary, Anne's sister. They come to me from historical research on the Internet, and in person in Ukraine, from my memory of my Grendys grandparents, and from Anne's treasured papers.

It is all of us, Callisons, Grendys, Moures, who can speak today and try to remember in our various ways, when Anne Callison can't tell us everything she knows (though she does remember it, and wants to impart it).

An acclaimed European poet from Galicia in Spain, Chus Pato, said to me once, when we were walking together in Ukraine through the village where Anne and her sister Mary were born, talking about the terrible crises of war and genocide in Europe in the 20th century: "People don't live history; they live their lives. History passes over them as catastrophe." In Canada and in the Peace River Country, in that same 20th century, history also passed over the Indigenous peoples, and over the newcomers who settled here from Europe and the United States. All in all, those newcomers also *participated* in history, and their decisions and actions played a role in what the Peace River country is today. That was exactly why our immigrant forebears came over such great distances and at such a personal cost to an unknown land: to have a chance to participate and make history and not just be dragged under by catastrophe.

At the same time, it has to be noted that, before the influx of European settlers in the lands of the North Peace, of the "tired and hungry and the huddled masses" mentioned in the poem engraved at the bottom of the American Statue of Liberty, there were already people living on this land for thousands of years. Their view of the "opportunity" provided by treaties and subsequent settlement was very different from that of the settlers, although they, too, lived their lives in the wish for peace and prosperity for their families and for the future. It seems fair to say that since the signing of the treaties in Canada in the late 19th century and early 20th century, the settler view of opportunity has dominated, and we are only beginning now to listen to the First Peoples as nations with views and rights, and knowledges of the land that we need to listen to, urgently.

This noted, however, ours is a humbler story, Anne's story, a settler story told from a woman's point of view, and valorizing the experience and viewpoint of a woman, Anne Callison, née Grendys.

Anne's story cannot be told, as she rightly insists, without the story of her husband John. So that's where we'll begin.

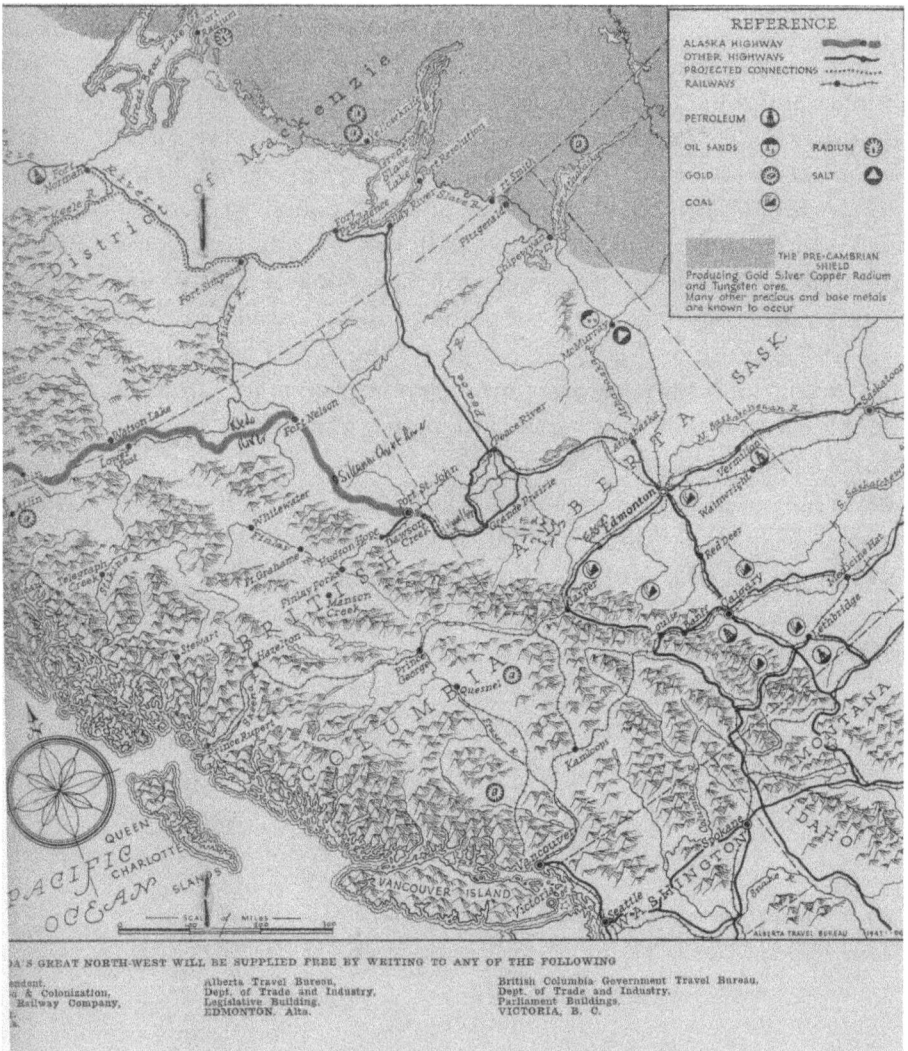

An early 20th century government map of the Peace River country, on which the Alaska Highway is drawn by hand.

John's Start

Halliday, North Dakota, USA to the North Peace District

In Anne Callison's cherished papers, on xeroxed copies of marriage records from a Callison family bible, we find the first mention of John Callison's father, Frederick C. Callison, in a looping script that states: "Fred C. Callison and Dora E. Lynch (Dora Elton Lynch) was married April 23, 1907." It is the third marriage listed in the bible; the first one on the list was in 1898, at the turn of the 20th century.

Curiously, or comically, scribbled on the verso side of the venerable photocopy are what appear to be cribbage scores, in Anne's writing. Just so you know, when it comes to having fun, Anne Callison leaves no scrap of paper unturned!

The Callisons, originally Irish immigrants, had been in America at least since the early 18th century; John's great grandfather, Colonel Elisha Callison, was born on April 17, 1792 in Tennessee and died July 27, 1852 in Lewisburg, West Virginia where he had settled to work as a drover. Fred Callison, one of the colonel's great-grandsons and John's father, was born on a plantation in West Virginia in 1885. After losing his father John Charles, sheriff of Green Briar County, and his mother to measles when he was seventeen, Fred headed west by train to work as a wrangler in the Dakotas. He returned to West Virginia four years later with money in his pocket and married Dora (Lynch) Muth, widow of Daniel Martin Muth, who had drowned near Alvon, West Virginia in 1902 when Dora was pregnant. Her son, Daniel Mohler Muth, had been born July 8, 1902. Dora Lynch—one of ten children of William Brownlee Lynch, a Confederate cavalry officer, and Elizabeth Virginia Blair—was born January 20, 1879 in Greenbriar County, West Virginia.

The couple returned west to Halliday, North Dakota with young Dan and homesteaded; with the homestead proved up in 1907, they took up cattle ranching. John Frederick Callison was born in Halliday in 1909, joining his elder brother Lynch (born in 1908 and named for his mother's family). John's birth was followed by that of Edward Patrick (Pat) in 1910, and of Norma in 1912. There is an early photo of John in

North Dakota, a small toddler outside a sod house, his clothes muddy, his face looking outward.

After a few years of droughts and tornadoes, Fred went alone to the Peace River Country in 1911 to check out rumours about new homesteads on fertile prairie, where a railway was about to arrive. While there, Fred registered for a homestead on the Pouce Coupe prairie (named after Thomas Puskupy, a local Dane-zaa man), near where he thought the promised railway would pass.

In March the next year, when John was four, and with Norma[1] born, the Fred Callison family packed their belongings onto two horse-drawn sleighs and headed north to Peace River country, via Portal, North Dakota/Saskatchewan and then by train to Spirit River, Alberta and onward by horseback and covered wagon to the Pouce Coupe plain near Dawson Creek to take up their homestead. Since they knew the region well and where supplies could be had, they opened a store, which they ran from a tent; they built barns, sheds, planted a garden.

Settled in Canada, the family grew. In 1914, Elisha Oscar (Lash) was the first white boy born on that prairie. Soon after, far away from the North Peace, western Europe erupted in a war that, because of colonization and alliances, became the first World War. The tenant on the Callison ranch in North Dakota having left to fight in Europe, the family returned to North Dakota to care for their vacant ranch. After the war, in 1918, the Spanish flu epidemic nearly took Fred's life; all the family except Dora caught it. In 1919, with everyone recovered, the family was able to return to the Pouce Coupe prairie and homestead, with six boys now and two girls, as Doris was born in 1916, and the twins Dennis[2] and Daisy[3] in 1919. Mollie was born in Canada, in 1924, rounding out Dora's family, and Fred's first one. Dan Muth, Dora's first child, at some point returned to live in the USA with an aunt in Pasadena, and later emigrated to New Zealand.[4]

Throughout the 1920s, Fred, a man of hard work and resilience, held contracts for several road and rail building projects. Horses were

---

[1] died January 1, 2007.

[2] d. March 19, 2007.

[3] d. May 21, 2013.

[4] Dora went once, in 1935, from the Peace River down to the Pasadena, USA to visit her dying mother. She arrived a few days late. She did not see Dan again.

required to pull road-building machinery, and he and his sons could handle horses. John and his brothers went to work for a living in 1921 when John was 12, building grade with their father for the new railway between Wembley and Hythe, Alberta. They worked ten hours a day for $4, quite a sum at the time! As Lash said in a newspaper years later: "there was no overtime, compensation, coffee breaks, or running water. We furnished our own tent and bedroll and slept on the ground."[5]

Early on, John Callison began trapping with his father and brothers. His Dad Fred, it is said, was taught by a Métis trapper named Alex Gladue, who had come to the Pouce Coupe area following the Riel Rebellion in Manitoba. The income from trapping was critical to keeping the family solvent, especially since the promised railway—necessary for shipping grain—was delayed by the steel needs of war. Trapping was to become a major part of John's life; it kept him and his brothers going with dignity during the Great Depression, when the world economy failed due to the actions of capital and politics, and ordinary people who lived in cities were bereft of work, money, and often of food. The price of furs was buoyant, though, and trappers made a good living in those times.

The place where the Callisons first came, at the south end of Swan Lake near Pouce Coupe, had been opened up to settlement in 1912, after the First Nations of the area, Dane-zaa people known then as the Fort St. John Beaver, adhered to Treaty 8 in 1900 (later becoming the Doig River First Nation and Blueberry River First Nation). The Hudson Hope Beaver adhered to Treaty 8 in 1914 (later the Halfway River First Nation). Dane-zaa traditional territory extended to the Rocky Mountains in the West, and east and north across the great prairie into Alberta, through Hythe, Worsley, and other towns, and north to the Northwest Territories where the Peace River runs into the Athabaska and then the Slave and Mackenzie Rivers. Under the Treaty, however, they were granted but small territories for reserves where they gathered yearly and where they wintered, retaining the right to carry out their traditional culture on all their territory—now known as Crown Lands—including hunting, trapping, and fishing, gathering of plants and berries for food

---

[5] Callison file, *Fort St. John North Peace Museum Archives.* The elements of Callison history included here are drawn from articles held in this file. Most are yellowed newspaper clippings without clear dates or attribution.

and medicine, enacting of spiritual ceremonies tied to place and memory, and other activities.

When the first homesteads of the Peace River Block were open for claiming by newcomers, quarter sections (160 acres) could be had for $10.00. The homesteader was obliged to "prove up" the land, earning their land title by clearing trees, fencing, breaking the soil and planting crops, building a house and barn, and they had to live there for six months of the year.

The farmers, entrepreneurs and trappers who were the first settlers never questioned the Indigenous rights surrendered in the treaties, and didn't ever look into whether the rights that were retained were respected. They simply accepted their own right to settle in the area and farm, to sell and buy land, create roads and transport goods, hunt and trap, and to vote and live where they pleased. The relationship with Indigenous people was seen as the responsibility of the far-away Federal Government, "the Crown." Still, the newcomers did live in and among Indigenous people, in a land that at the time seemed largely boundless; they worked nearby and alongside each other, shared habits and knowledge, and in great part respected each other's assigned spaces. The region was isolated; opportunities for commerce were few, and all seized opportunities that came to them. First Nations peoples, though allocated reserves, ranged over the breadth of their traditional territories and lived their traditional ways wherever they were not kept out by farms; they spoke their languages and practised their spiritual traditions, while also participating in the fur trade and other new economic activities when it made sense to them and helped them preserve and protect their way of life.

We'll end this short look at John Callison's early years on the note of spiritual tradition, remembering that it was in the Bible of his Methodist mother where we first met the Callison family. John's faith was formed by his respect for life, nature, family, and the Creator who drew it all together to work in harmony. John had a sense of humility and almost of obligation to work harder and longer than others, always with unquestionable honesty. In these pages we recognize, simply, that the precepts of dignity, respect, peace, honesty, and fairness to all creatures, human or animal, were what guided John in his everyday behaviour, all his life.

Anne's Start
Velyki Hlibovychi, then Poland, now Ukraine, to Huallen, Alberta

In a video in 2006-2007, Anne Callison was interviewed as a senior and long-time resident of the North Peace[6] and spoke of her own family history and that of her husband John; she started by saying that her father was Austrian.

Her father, Tom Grendys, did define himself as Austrian—and this is important: in the face of the fratricidal wars of the 20th century, he saw himself as a citizen of a great multicultural empire, not as a member of an ethnicity. Tomasz Grędysz (Томас Грендіс 1877-1977) was born in Chlebowice Wielkie, south of the Imperial city of Lemberg (today's Lviv), to Jan Grędysz and Maria Odzianska. A primarily Ukrainian village in the eastern part of the Galician province of the Austria-Hungarian Empire, Chlebowice Wielkie had long been ethnically mixed.[7] There was a Roman Catholic Church[8] and a Polish-language school, and a Greek Catholic Church and Ukrainian school. Tom married Anastasia Hamulyak (Анастасія Хамуляк, 1889-1963, also Chamulak in English), daughter of Alex Hamulyak, a prosperous farmer in the village, and Anna Bartkow. In that period, about 15% of marriages in eastern Galicia were mixed. This was the case for both Tom's marriage with Anastasia, who was Greek Catholic and considered herself Ukrainian, and for that of Anastasia's parents, for her mother's name was seen as Polish. After the Austrian Empire crumbled in the First World War, the area in which

---

[6] "Interview with Anne Callison, April 3, 2007, Fort St. John BC," on *Treasured Chronicles II: Thru the eyes of our North Peace Elders*, Interviewee Copy. Pouce Coupe, BC: Hill Computing Inc. DVD. Collection Anne Callison. Anne was one of 200 seniors who were interviewed as part of this project.

[7] In 1880, the village held 1637 people: 158 Roman Catholic, 1452 Greek Catholic, and 27 Jewish (*Słownik geograficzny Królestwa Polskiego i innych krajów słowiańskich, Tom I, 582*). The mix remained constant until the destructions of World War Two.

[8] Parish registers of Roman Catholic births and marriages for Chlebowice Wielkie, Galicia, Austria; later Chlebowice Wielkie (Bóbrka), Lwów, Poland; now Velyki Hlibovychi, L'viv, Ukraine, 1784-1941, are held on microfilm in the Mormon Family History Centre in Salt Lake City, Utah. Text in Latin and Polish.

the village lay was made part of Poland. Today the village is called Velyki Hlibovychi (Великих Глібович) and lies in Ukraine.

The Austro-Hungarian Empire existed before Eastern Europe was split into "ethnically homogenous" nations. This split, which had occurred earlier in Western Europe (and was very much imposed there as well) was much harder to enforce in the vast lands of the European East that had nourished mixed populations for hundreds of years.

Velyki Hlibovychi, Ukraine, from "Storonka," 2008.

Thus in the 20th century, as wars altered borders, and empires collapsed, these areas of mixed population were to endure a century of exiles and emigrations, then of genocides, forced migrations, ethnic cleansing, and banishment, in order to make them "reliable" for the new state and mono-ethnic governments that arose. It sounds terrible and was, but people in that 20th century believed for a long time (and some still believe) that only by separating all national groups could war be avoided and peoples controlled. Meanwhile, in Canada and the USA, mixed populations who came and lived together based on shared values of security, human rights, prosperity, and respect (though also with colonial attitudes toward the land they lived on), flourished.

The emigrations from those Eastern lands, including those of the Grędysz and Hamulyak families from Chlebowice-Hlibovychi, held both sadness at what was left behind, and hope for what was to come.

The sadness was one reason that the emigrants' most common name for their place of origin was "the Old Country." Often people did not even know what country it was; the borders had so often shifted. As well, in those days, people's sense of identity came from their village and church, not yet from a single "national" origin.

Normally, in mixed villages, daughters would be baptized in the church of the mother, and sons in that of the father, unless the family didn't like the priest and went to the other religion. Thus in Velyki Hlibovychi, as elsewhere, there were also folks called Latynnyky (латинників) in the census, who though baptized as Roman Catholic not Greek Catholic, still identified as Ukrainian. A few dozen Jewish people also lived in the village, and some also intermarried; some of them may have been related to the Grendys. No wonder Tom Grendys, as he was known in Canada, declared that he was Austrian!

VIGNETTE: The Birth Certificate

One day as a small girl, I, being the daughter of Anne's sister Mary, unearthed my mother's birth certificate among her papers. I was always trying to find things to read. My mother had long told me, in answer to the question "where do you come from, Mom?" that she came from "nowhere." Or from "Hythe, Alberta." (For some reason she preferred not to say Huallen, which was actually the closest population point.) But on this day, I showed my mother the certificate, written in Old Latin and headed "Republic of Poland." Mom! I said, look! You come from somewhere! You come from Poland! My Mom looked at the paper with puzzlement and said: "That's not right. I don't come from Poland. I don't know why it says that." "But where do you come from?" "The Old Country," my mother said. And then: "I come from Ukraine. My mother was Ukrainian," she said.[9]

---

[9] https://uk.wikipedia.org/wiki/Великі_Глібовичі The village is located in the Peremyshlyan district, 6.6 km west of the town of Bibrka, itself 20 km SE of Lviv. It stretches along the river Davydivka, which flows north to south into the Dniester. The village is 15 km long and divided into neighbourhoods: **Задвір**, "Zadvir" (once a separate village), **Горіше**," Horish," up the hill, **Доліше**, "Dolishee," in the valley, and **Сторонка**, "Storonka" or "Side," located on the other side of the river. The first mention of the village dates back to 1442. See the appendix for more on the difficult history of the village in the 20th century.

The young Grędysz couple, Tom and Anastasia, likely resided at the farm of Anastasia's father, Alex. Land ownership records in the Lviv Archives indicate where the Hamulyaks owned land in the village. The Grędysz families, for their part, lived on the other side of the river Davydivka, and did not have lands or cattle, only houses and gardens. Alex Hamulyak, unlike many Ukrainian farmer-peasants, did have land. Most land around the village, however, was in the hands of the historical Polish landlords, the *pani* or lords, of which there was one smaller landowner, Leon Urbanski, and one from the noble Potocki family, Alfred Potocki. Nearly everyone in the village spoke both Polish and Ukrainian and a mixture of the two that Anne's sister Mary called "village language." Jewish neighbours would have spoken Yiddish too.

The first children of the young Grędysz couple were fraternal twins, Jan (later John) and Leon (later Leo), born in 1910. A few months later, father Tom, who had already served in the Austro-Hungarian Imperial army, fearing war and being called into service again,[10] emigrated from the village with other family heads who were around his age, Jan Horbal and Iwan Mazur, plus a married woman named Warwara Glowacka (Barbara Glowacki) with a 10 month old baby named Iwan (Ivan or John), and a teenager named Michal Kalitan.

They arrived on April 11, 1911 at Ellis Island in the New York City harbour, on board the ship Finland from Antwerp. They saw the Statue of Liberty for the first time, and entered the USA as landed immigrants. Tomasz Grendysz, as his name was now spelled in American English, was recorded in the landing books as being 29 years old, able to read and write, Polish in ethnicity, married, a labourer by profession, with a cousin in Auburn NY, and a citizen of Chlebowice, Austria (as the village was then in the Austro-Hungarian Empire, Austria for short). Jan Horbal was listed as Ruthenian (Ukrainian), married, a farm labourer,

---

[10] I remember riding in the dark in my parents' car back from Saskatoon Mountain to Grande Prairie with Grandpa Tom, sometime in the mid 1960s. I asked him why he had come to Canada. "No war," he replied. "In Old Country, always armies. One army, another army. In the army, they send you to shoot your brothers. In Canada, no war." In 2008, when I went to the village, a woman who had Grendys ancestry (her great-grandma was grandpa's sister) told me the road outside where the Grendys had once lived was called the "soldiers' road." Armies marched past and pressed men into service. Sometimes brothers ended up in opposing armies. Armies also set up camp in the fields, and left crops trampled.

and 27 years old. Barbara Glowacki was listed as 23 years old, married, and Ruthenian, and as being unable to read and write. Michal Kalitan was listed as Polish, single, and 19 years old. Iwan Mazur was 34, married, and Polish.

Tom Grendys, as he quickly became known, dropping the Polish endings of his name, came with $26, and was headed to 113 State Street, Auburn NY where his cousin Jana Grendysa lived. Others were headed to Auburn as well.

Today the site of that house in Auburn is a parking lot next to a river and railway track, across from which is a large prison. In the other direction, a few streets away, is Perrine Street, where Tom Grendys's older sister's granddaughter Olga Gelembiuk lived until her death in 2013. This area of Auburn, Olga told me in 2003 (when I visited "the American cousins" with my mother) held many people both Polish and Ukrainian from the Old Country. No one had gone back. Olga remembered times of animosity there: Polish and Ukrainian Americans often wouldn't even walk on the same side of the street, so strong was the inherited enmity between the two cultures, given in particular the recurrent valiant but failed attempts by Ukrainians to have their own state free of Polish authority, and given the inter-war Polish repressions.

1907, industry in Auburn NY, to show you how the town bustled!

In Auburn, in the northwest part of New York state, Eastern Europeans were welcome as immigrants in the early 20th century. In 1890, state prisoners had ceased to be used for outside labour (though they continue to this day to work for the state making license plates).

Auburn, full of factories founded on river-driven electric power and access to prison labour, had to source new workers, and welcomed the immigrants from Austro-Hungary. Tom Grendys, who very likely, it seems, worked in his native village as a blacksmith, was able to transfer his metalworking skills to work in Auburn. One wonders if he might have worked in the Auburn Works of the International Harvester Company making farm machinery! No record remains of the details of his work, so we can only guess.

Just before World War I, on May 26, 1914, Tom was joined in the USA by Anastasia, who left their twin sons at home in the village. Her father Alex, initially against the emigration, had relented and given them his blessing to leave, but he wanted to have heirs to farm. Anastasia's entry in the register at Ellis Island, on the ship Vaterland from Antwerp, misspells her name as "Anastarya Grandysz" from "Chtebowice, Austria." It states that she was 24 years old and married, could read and write, and her nearest relative in Chlebowice was her father, Oleksy Chamulak (Alex Hamulyak); she was a housewife by profession, going to Auburn NY, to 115 State Street, where her husband Tomasz Grendysz lived. Marya Podzikowski, from the same village, and 26 years old, arrived with her, though her final destination was Chicago.[11]

In 1915 in Auburn, Alexander was born. By 1918, when Josef was born, they lived in Cleveland, Ohio, where Tomasz worked for River Furnace smelting pig iron, alongside his wife's sister's husband. Anastazyja or Anastasia, known as Nelly now, pined after her twin sons John and Leo whom she'd left in Europe. She missed her father Alex, too, whose health was failing. But war still raged in Eastern Europe. After the 1918 armistice in the West, in the void left in the East by the

---

[11] Other Grendysz and Hamulyak family members emigrated to the area of Auburn and northern New York State, and to Cleveland. There was, at least, a brother of Anastasia, and a child of Tom's sister Anna, or perhaps Anna herself. My mother kept in touch with cousins Patricia (Clarke, later of Washington State) and Alex, both children of her mother's brother Alex Hamulyak, and with Olga Gelembiuk (née Mulyk), granddaughter of her father's sister Anna. The names were later spelled variously: Hamulak, Humuliak, Hamulack, Humulock. Grendysz became Grendys, but also, at times, Grandish. Very hard to tell now who is actually related. But, for the record, cousin Lt. Col. Alexander A. Humulock Jr (son of Ukrainian immigrant Alexander Hamulack and Zofea Zlotorowicz of Ithaca), born January 29, 1925 in Ithaca NY, died December 2, 2015, in Romulus, NY. Cousin Olga Gelembiuk, born May 24, 1922, died May 14, 2013 in Auburn, NY.

collapse of the Austro-Hungarian Empire, Poles and Ukrainian insurgent armies were still at war. Ukrainians, unhappy that the treaty of Versailles failed to recognize their nation and give them a country, fought the Poles, who were determined to control all Galicia, east and west. The League of Nations, forerunner of the United Nations, declared on February 23, 1921 that Galicia was not part of Poland and that the fate of Poland's military occupation of Eastern Galicia, where the great city of Lviv (Lemberg, Lvov, Lwow) and the Grendys village lay, would be determined later.

In the hope of peace, the Grendys family returned to Chlebowice Wielkie. The political situation was still uncertain, as the West Ukrainian Republic government was in exile and Poland still occupied the area. On March 14, 1923, the League of Nations decided that Eastern Galicia would be incorporated into Poland, with recognition that Ukrainians, the majority in the area, deserved autonomous status and land grants, which Poland promised to fulfill. Once the West Ukrainian government had disbanded, however, Poland reneged on its promises.

1921 passport photo, Cleveland Ohio: with American-born sons Alex and Joe.

The Grędysz family was now back in their village, with the Hamulyaks, and reunited with their twin sons. The couple rejoiced at the birth of their first daughter, Anna, on December 15, 1921. Three years later, on November 27, 1924, the youngest in the family, Marja, or Mary, was born in house 211 on Hamulyak land in the village, not far from the Ukrainian school.[12]

Meanwhile, the lost war led to an upsurge of Ukrainian resistance in the area, and violence was never far from brewing. Animosity between Polish State and frustrated Ukrainian citizenry was increasing. Instead of granting autonomy as they had agreed under the treaty, the Polish state enacted a policy of assimilation and repression of Ukrainian populations. Use of the Ukrainian language was banned in government agencies in 1924 and support withdrawn from Ukrainian schools. Though his wife wanted to stay in their traditional lands, Tom Grendys dreamed of leaving again for America. Feeling that war was sure to return, he wanted only to take his family far from any possibility of destruction.

Approx. location of Mary's birth, Hamulyak farm; Velyki Hlibovychi, 2011 (buildings not the same today).

---

[12] In 2008-9, my friends did research in the Lviv archives for me. On analysis of old village maps, they were able to identify the land Alex Hamulyak owned, and the location of their house in the village. Thanks to Oksana and Taras Dudko. I have made visits to the village on three occasions: in 2008, 2009, and 2011.

Both Alex and Josef went to school in the village, in Polish, as dictated by the state. As Joe Grendys remembered years later, the Polish School was beside the Polish (Roman Catholic) Church, at a crossroads with the Ukrainian (Greek Catholic) church and school across the road. In Polish school, the two boys would be assimilated as Polish. Their father, Tom, continued to think of himself as Austrian. Alex Hamulyak, after long illness, died in 1929. With the money Anastasia realized from sale of her share of the estate, the Grendys were able to afford to pay the family's passage back to America.

Former Polish school. Velyki Hlibovychi, 2008, where Joe Grendys went.

This time, however, their return was not to the USA, for an immigration law passed in 1924 had drastically restricted the entry of Eastern Europeans, and banned entry of anyone from Asia. The law had undertones of anti-Semitism, as many immigrants from Eastern Europe earlier in the century and now established had been Jewish. Officially, it was claimed that the law aimed to maintain a "Nordic" ethnic homogeneity. So the Grendys family found themselves unable to return to the country where they had first settled and where two of their children were born.

In 1929, another possibility for emigration emerged, in letters written home by fellow villagers. The Peace River District west of Grande Prairie, Alberta, in Canada, had been very affected by the drop in wheat prices in the early 1920s. Farmers of those rich soils, who had settled early in the century after the signing of Treaty 8, had to pay much higher prices than farmers on the Canadian Prairies to ship wheat to the ports at the head of Lake Superior. With the drop in wheat prices, many settlers on more marginal land, especially, were forced to abandon their homesteads to seek work elsewhere. In the late 1920s, the government began to reallocate these empty homesteads, hoping for tax revenue again. Harry Glowaski, a fellow villager from Chlebowice who had emigrated to Canada on June 11, 1927 (his fare was $250—a fortune in those times!) on his own, leaving his wife of two years behind, happened to be there. Working in sawmills and on farms, from Winnipeg west through various places in Alberta, and sending money home, Harry had not yet found a permanent place to settle. Then he met Stanislaw Kasprow, a friend and earlier immigrant from Chlebowice, who talked him into heading to Wembley, Alberta, in the South Peace. So it was that in early 1929, Harry Glowaski filed for his own homestead for $10 in the area of Mountain Side, northeast of Saskatoon Mountain, at 17.79.7.W6. He also claimed a homestead for Tom Grendys and his wife Anastazyja, on top of the mountain on the NW quarter of Sec.14 Twp.72 Rge.9 W6; beside the Stan Kasprow's land (NE quarter).

Tomasz and Anastazyja Grędysz, now with four robust sons and two young daughters, left their village of Chlebowice just after May 6, 1929, destined for their new Canadian home west of Grande Prairie and north of Huallen, where they would become farmers.

Anastazyja and Tom (Tomasz, Tomi) with Anna, Marja, and Josef, May 1929. Passport photo for their journey to Canada, taken in Bobrka, Poland (now Bibrka, Ukraine). Marja, later Mary, never liked this photo as her father's face was obscured by the Canadian Immigration stamp! Alex, Jan, and Leon would have had their own passports. The photographer Isak Messer, and his entire family of printers and photographers, were murdered in Bobrka in 1943 in the Holocaust. (In the area south of Lviv (Lemberg) where the Grendys came from, only 1 man in 5, and 2 women in 5, survived the Second World War.)

The family arrived in Halifax from Antwerp via Liverpool on June 1, 1929, and were admitted as Polish in nationality (their village was at this point in Poland), with their name spelled as Grendysz. It is noteworthy that "ethnicity" in the records had now become "nationality," referring to citizenship rather than ethnic origin and language. They came as farmers, and entered Canada with $600 to their name, which was about a year of income in those days. The last leg of their train journey west was on the colonist cars of Northern Alberta Railways. Arrived in Hythe, the brand new end-point of the railway, they took hired horse-drawn wagons over the muddy roads and up Saskatoon Mountain to their homestead.

Anastazyja Grendysz—Anastasia or Nelly in Canada—planted her own garden plus a first garden for Mrs. Glowaski, who came later that summer. The families started to clear land to plant hay and grain, using axes, pulling trees to the edges with horses, and picking stones and roots by hand. Building a house was a priority. In the gardens, women planted root vegetables for winter storage, as well as summer leaf vegetables, and cabbages for preserving in barrels as sauerkraut. Wild berries were gathered as well.

On July 28, 1929, Mrs. Glowaski and their two daughters, Stella and Anna, arrived from the village and the Glowaskis settled on their quarter section north of Wembley, where they lived till 1963. They farmed at first, as reported by Harry Glowaski, with a walking plough, then with a horse-drawn breaking plough. They grew oats and wheat, and had cattle, hogs, chickens, geese, ducks, and turkeys. Their first tractor, when they could afford one, was a John Deere Model M, purchased years later, in 1947. The following two quotes from a community memoir tell a story of the Glowaskis that very likely could have been told of the Grendys family.

> There were only the bare necessities for furnishings in the small three room log house. The first years of seeding and harvesting were all done by hand. The grain crop was harvested by scythe and sickle, dried and flailed and the chaff blown by sifting grain in the wind. It was bagged and taken to the flour mill at Sexsmith. The small income was that from the sales of grain, hogs, and cattle, supplemented by Mr. Glowaski working on farms in the area. Often there was no cash, so butter, eggs, etc. were traded at Mrs. Kranz's store in Wembley for staples such as sugar, salt, baking powder and so on. Clothing was sewn by hand with material purchases through Eatons or Simpsons catalogues. Transportation was by sleigh, wagon or foot. It was eight

miles into Wembley for the mail and groceries. All the neighbours in the area helped each other out, and depended on each other.[13]

Early residents saw Indian wagons travel to the island in Saskatoon Lake even after the surrounding land was homesteaded. The Indians brought most of their possessions with them, and travelled with their families on a low wagon or cart drawn by a team of ponies, with any extra possessions behind on a travois. At the Island they would set up teepees and stay for a few days or weeks when the saskatoon berries were ripening. They dried these berries in the sun and they were kept for winter food. They held a celebration as well at the island in the 1920s, a powwow with dancing and with tomtoms, in mid-summer. They received their treaty money at this time. After the 1929 celebration, it was learned that smallpox had struck the Indian people and some of their people in the park developed the disease that year; two died.[14]

On arrival, with the help of others, the Grendys family built a log house with two storeys. This house, fallen down, still existed in the early 1960s (I remember being told to stay out of the ruins so as not to get hurt). Later in the 1930s, they had built a more modern two-storey farmhouse. There was a well near the house with a hand-pump for delicious fresh water, and outhouses for sanitary purposes. Coal-oil lamps were used to light the house, and Nelly cooked on a woodstove. The main floor of the new house, which was inhabited right through the 1960s, held kitchen, pantries, and dining area on one side, and the living room on the other. Upstairs was the sleeping space for the family. At some point, an entryway was built over the door at the side of the house, and there was a small hand-pump for water, a "sink" that was a bowl set into a wooden counter, for washing up on coming into the house, and a butter churn. When you came in, you'd wash your hands and crank the butter churn a few times.

Anne Grendys would walk or ride with her younger sister Mary to school down the mountain. Anne remembered that she always walked

---

[13] *Lake Saskatoon Reflections: A Local history of the Lake Saskatoon district*, Sexsmith AB: Lake Saskatoon History Book Committee, 1980, 146.

[14] *Lake Saskatoon Reflections*, p. 21 and 164. Another local family from the village was Hrychiw, who farmed SW22.72.9.W6 on Saskatoon Mountain. John Hrychiw and family of Wembley sent condolences and flowers after Anastasia Grendys's death in 1963. When the Hrychiw family arrived in 1930, they stayed with nearby friends, apparently. These might have been Grendys or Kasprow.

slower than her sister, who was fast on her feet. Anne looked out for her little sister as much as she could. Their school was called Mountain Trail, and opened in 1930 about three miles (5 km) south down the mountain toward the village of Huallen. At first, the girls walked as much as six miles to get to school, as there was no road down the mountain. The teacher soon reported that this was much too far, and a trail was cut to meet a rural road that led south to the school, which stood at the intersection with a road that was once part of the Dane-zaa trail between Grande Prairie, Pouce Coupe, and Dawson Creek. Mountain Trail School was built of logs by a group of parents, and was plastered and painted on the inside; it had a wall of windows facing East, to catch the morning light. A stable was built on the corner of the property, as many students arrived on horseback. At the school, Anne did well, and she remembers that the teacher taught her that she was capable of doing anything. She got as far as Grade 7, then her mother had major surgery and needed Anne's help around the house as she recovered. After that, Anne just kept working on the farm to help her mom. She harboured other dreams, though!

Her sister Mary loved school and was so independent, she was hard to keep at home. She wouldn't sit still in school, and the teacher used to call Mary "the wandering Jew" for her restlessness. She told me that her feet always hurt from wearing second-hand shoes, so she only wore them at school and rode to school wearing her socks only. I once asked her if she ever told her mother about the shoes. "No," said Mary, "she had enough to worry about." Mary continued to go to school at Mountain Trail through Grade 8, then stayed an additional year to do Grade 9 by correspondence and have help from the teacher, so that she could go to High School in Grande Prairie. The priest in the area encouraged her, and helped find her a family where she could board in Grande Prairie. There, Mary did housework and cooking in return for room and board while studying. The nuns at St. Joseph's High School paid for Mary's books. Mary became a registered nurse after the war (there was a shortage of nurses and tuition was free at the Edmonton General Hospital, and the nuns paid for her books, uniforms, and tests in exchange for extra work in the wards). She worked in the health field all her life. Mary remembered that Mountain Trail school was a hub for social events, school plays, and seasonal celebrations for the parents and children; it was a centre of activity and of sharing news. She said that even though many parents were immigrants from Eastern Europe, they always spoke English at the school as, particularly in the 1930s, there were rumours of immigrants being deported to Russia, whether or not they were Russian! Obviously, that story frightened people. Another story Mary told me was of her habit of falling asleep on her horse on the way home from school. The horse, King (a foundling rescued by their Dad after its mother was hit by a train), knew where to go. Once, though, Mary woke up in the trees, still on her horse, to the sound of voices calling her name in the dark! The horse was just waiting quietly. How on earth did King get there? Mary never knew; she figured the horse had seen a bear and bolted to get away, while she was fast asleep! Her family had been in a panic when they hadn't come home, and had gathered the neighbours and gone out to search for them.

Anne speaks in glowing terms of her brothers and her Dad. They worked hard, she said. Alex, and Leo and John, who were older, left early in their homesteading years for the East, "right after arriving," said her sister Mary. They rode the freight trains as men did during the Depression, in search of work. They believed that opportunities would be better *off* the farm, and Alex and Joe were both American citizens by birth, so could return. Joe did go East at one point, but returned as his father wrote him to request his help on the farm. John took a lot of trips east, back and forth on the train. Alex, as well, would return for visits. He was always a fan of automobiles and many photos show him standing beside one! He became a machinist in Ithaca, NY and as he worked for NCR, National Cash Register, he always had money in his pocket to go out, and to buy cars. It is said Alex was popular with the girls! He told my brother Bill his popularity was due to his having some coins in his pockets, as this was during the Depression. Alex looked out for his older brothers Leo and John. John had gone East to work and live, and at one point worked for Alex as a handyman at Alex's Spring Water Motel in Ithaca, NY.[15] Joe, as his father wished, returned to work the farm.

"My Dad was a good Dad," says Anne. "He was working all the time, and my brother Joe worked with him." "I'd help look after my sister, and help my mother. I was pretty young." Anne remembers that they had lots of food, a root cellar full of vegetables to keep them

---

[15] Motel as listed in 1958 *Manning's Ithaca Directory*, 425: "Spring Water Motel, Mr. and Mrs. Alex A. Grendys, props. Dryden Rd, Route 18, Varna." The motel has been enlarged and still exists in 2017 as the Embassy Inn.

through the winter, as well as chickens, ducks, turkeys, pigs, and cows for milk. "No one worried in the winter," Anne said. "The house was warm, and there was lots to eat." Her father hunted a bit as well, and she'd go out hunting with him and her brothers for deer.

Summer was beautiful. The family had 10 to 20 cows, for milk. And they made cheese. Anne says they must have made sausage, *kulbassa*, but she doesn't remember a smokehouse. "Mom had birds," she said, "chickens and turkeys. She'd kill them and we'd eat that."

Both she and her sister Mary said that they didn't eat the butter they produced, but brought it to town to sell door to door. With the cash, during the Depression, the family was able to buy salt, sugar, and baking powder: the few supplies that their farm did not provide.

When asked about whether her father Tom had a "still," for distilling alcohol, Anne said she didn't remember that he had one. Her sister did tell me stories of a home distillery, hidden in a hole in a barn, so that when the Mounties showed up looking for illegal alcohol, the sour smell was masked by the smell of pig manure! I am not sure now, however, if Mary was speaking of her father or of other heads of family. Mary did tell me that the production of alcohol was at times a problem for families, as the alcohol was sometimes too strong and killed the drinker, or the still caught fire, and burned down buildings! Whatever operation their father had, if he indeed had one, it was small and carefully shepherded; though illegal in Canada, home distilling was a normal part of farm and village life in the Old Country.

"The best thing that happened to us," recounted Anne, "was the Indians." She remembers, as a child, being offered what she first thought was water, and it turned out to be tea. "It was really good tasting tea, I really loved it; the Indians had the best tea. I don't know, I think it was made from sunflowers. It was made just *really* good." I asked her which nations the native people came from who lived around Saskatoon Mountain in Alberta and, later, around Montney BC in the North Peace. "I don't know, " replied Anne. "They were just people. They lived near us, but not on a farm." When asked where they lived, Anne (affected by aphasia) replied, "They lived in a place to stay." One place to which she could be referring is the Fort St. John Reserve, situated near Montney, which was the first reservation allocated to the Dane-ẕaa. The name of their chief Muckethay, in a corrupted English version, had become the name of the creek and of the district. Or she could be referring to the Dane-ẕaa who had a reserve near Horse Lake, west of Hythe near the Grendys family farm, in an area that was one of their traditional territories. They would come up the trails alongside the farm to pick berries on Saskatoon Mountain in the summer.[16]

We'll return to Montney later in the book, but Anne did remember First Nations fellows working for them and helping them at Murdale. Her memories are warm ones. Relationships between Indigenous and settler peoples were complex for those who experienced them.[17] On one hand, they were guided by an aboriginal ethics of hospitality and peace when people treated each other fairly. At the same time, administrative relations were fraught, marked by consternation and suffering at displacement from traditional territories, and lack of protection for treaty rights.

In books, the Dane-ẕaa refer to the settlers as "the newcomers," who make farms and just stay in one place.[18] Anne's sister Mary remembered that native people, known to white people in those days simply as "Indians," helped their father as well, not just to farm but to survive. Mary also remembered the medicine woman, who would come—with a child as interpreter—to stand on the road, waiting to be asked to help her mother with natural remedies when someone in the family was ill. She told me: "You always knew you were really sick if you looked out the window and the Indian doctor was there." "How did they know someone was sick?" I asked her. My mother looked surprised, as if I'd missed the point. "They lived there," she said, "so they knew."

---

[16] My mother (Mary) told me that there was an "Indian Trail" past the house, and said it led to places where the women would pick saskatoons in August. I remember as a child going with my aunt and cousin and my Mom to pick saskatoons for pie. The Horse Lake First Nation still exists, but removed "Beaver" (Dane-ẕaa) from their name years ago, as many members these days are part Cree.

[17] See Brenda Marie Ireland. *"Working a Great Hardship on Us": First Nations People, the State, and Fur Conservation in British Columbia before 1935* (UBC History Thesis, 1995) for a detailed history of administrative practices and relations.

[18] *Where Happiness Dwells: A History of the Dane-ẕaa First Nations.* Vancouver: UBC Press, 2013. See words of elder Tommy Attachie, Doig River First Nation, 244-5.

Gat Tah Kwâ

The Land of Those Who Dreamed

Dawson Creek, Fort St. John, and Old Fort Nelson (*Tthek'eneh Kúe*) were areas that knew and sheltered communities of people long before the settlers came from Europe and the United States. Their story holds material for many books, and they must have a place in the story of Anne and John Callison. It is not right to speak of "pioneers" without speaking of the valiant peoples who, under duress and worry at the incursion of the mostly white newcomers, surrendered lands to the abstract entity called "the Crown" in order to maintain their livelihoods and cultures, and who suffered greatly in consequence.

For more than 10,000 years, Dane-ẕaa (Beaver), Tsek'ene (Sekani), Dene Tha' (Slave), and other Dene peoples shared traditional territories in the region of the North Peace, and at times their territories overlapped somewhat, or shifted with the westward progress of the fur trade. Territory belonged to people by virtue of use, custom, and history, both spiritual and practical. Prior to arrival of the first Europeans, Cree and Métis traders arrived as intermediaries, introducing firearms, iron knives, matches, metal traps, flour, tea, and other goods from far away. When the first European traders arrived, local people participated with them in the fur trade. Being adaptable, they adopted European novelties when appropriate, and participated in related economies such as provision of meat to trading posts. They adopted horses in the late 19th century, and in the 1950s, with seismic crews cutting networks of rough roads into the bush, began to use wagons to access their territories, instead of riding or walking. It was the mid 1960s before trucks began to be used for hunting and travel to hunting camps, quite often in the form of a "band truck" bought for the whole nation.

In their ethos of custodianship of the land, and with an eye to the lives of their children, Indigenous nations signed treaties at the turn of the 20th century, which they believed were meant to share the wealth of the land, in return for protecting their traditional ways of living and caring for the land. They had already seen how the newcomers could decimate food supplies by overhunting, and could see that they would be powerless to turn away farmers, police, and railways. They knew the

33

land held oil, too, and could see that the newcomers were interested in it. Best to live in peace.

In the North Peace, in 1916, after entering into Treaty 8 with the Crown, the Dane-zaa in the area of Fort St. John were allotted twenty-eight sections of land in the Montney area: the St. John Indian Reserve No. 172.[19] This was their summer meeting place, for at other times of year, they still lived their traditional life over all of their traditional territory, carrying out activities protected by the treaty: trapping, hunting, gathering berries and medicinal plants, and maintaining sacred places and the stories held by keepers of the past and future known as the Dreamers.

The Dane-zaa consented to the sale of their reserve near Fort St. John in 1945, under pressure from the Federal Government which wanted to grant the lands to war veterans so they could farm the rich loam of the prairie there. The Dane-zaa people were mostly concerned at that time with preserving their traditional way of life in the face of the radical change brought by the Alaska Highway. It had created a situation of crisis for them in many ways, bringing diseases and cutting the migration routes of the animals they relied on for food during the long winters.

With proceeds of the sale, the Federal Department of Indian Affairs eventually bought reserve land further north for the Dane-zaa, in an area not rich for farming but closer to their trapping areas, which in themselves had been regulated in the 1930s by the introduction of a registration system which restricted their movements and assigned traplines in their traditional territory to white settlers as well.[20]

Unknowingly, the nation lost its mineral rights to the Montney land. When oil and gas were discovered on the former Dane-zaa reserve in 1976 (exploration began in the late 1940s), revenues went to the veterans

---

[19] http://calverley.ca/article/01-125-the-st-john-reserve-agricultural-settlement/ from *01-125: The "St. John Reserve" Agricultural Settlement* by Dorthea Calverley. "In 1904 the Indian Affairs Department arranged for this band to move to an area 10 miles north of Fort St. John but it was not until 1914 that the 18,000 acres was officially set up as a reserve, designated Montney Indian Reserve #172—later called the St. John Reserve."

[20] In *Maps and Dreams* (1982), ethnologist Hugh Brody explains how registration altered relations between First Nations and newcomers, ignoring rights protected by Treaty 8, allowing newcomers vast use of resources and restricting First Nations access to resources needed for their livelihoods, without consultation.

VIGNETTE: *Gat Tah Kwą̂, Chief Montney, and the Dane-zaa People*

"*Gat Tah Kwą̂* is the Dane-zaa land that lies just north of the city of Fort St. John. The name means "Spruce Among Houses," which refers to the large number of teepees our people had here both before and after Europeans came to our land. Montney Creek runs through Gat Tah Kwą̂. This creek, and the agricultural community now located here, were named after our Chief Montney. He died here in 1918, at the age of seventy-two, during the Spanish flu epidemic that ravaged our people. Our dancing grounds at Gat Tah Kwą̂ are called Suunéch'ii Kéch'iige, which means "The Place Where Happiness Dwells." Elders such as May Apsassin, Tommy Attachie and Madeline Davis remember how our people would gather there every summer to court, celebrate births, settle political issues, visit with relatives, and to drum, sing, and dance.

"The Dreamer Gaayęą named one of his songs "Suunéch'ii Kéch'iige." When our songkeepers sing that song now, it reminds us of the importance of the Dreamers' Dances we held there. Gaayęą died at Gat Tah Kwą̂ in 1923 after falling off of a horse, and we continue to care for his grave here and follow his teachings."

"We call our language *Dane-zaa Záágé?* which translates as "people-regular language" in English. It is also known as the Beaver Language, because of the name the Europeans gave our people during the fur trade."

"Until the mid-1950s, we lived a semi-nomadic lifestyle. We travelled seasonally within our Peace River country from the Rocky Mountains to the plains of Alberta to hunt, gather, and socialize with other Dane-zaa kinship groups.

In 1794, Rocky Mountain Fort was established in our traditional territories, and we began to participate in the fur trade. As a result of the fur trade, European culture slowly started to impact our traditional way of living. In 1900 we signed Treaty 8 an effort to preserve our lands and natural resources from outside interests. By 1914, we were allotted reserve land at Gat Tah Kwą̂ (Montney), one of our traditional gathering places, but for several decades we continued to travel freely throughout our traditional land.

During World War II, the US Army Corps of Engineers constructed the Alaska Highway across our traditional territory. After the war, the highway allowed an influx of settlers and developers to come into our land, and our lifestyle changed dramatically. We were forced to settle on reserves and to send our children to government schools. The Department of Indian Affairs agreed to sell our first reserve at Gat Tah Kwą̂ to the Department of Veterans' Affairs, and we were forced to move further north, to the land on Hanás̱ Saahgé? (Doig River), where our community is centred today."[21] [22]

---

[21] This vignette quotes from www.virtualmuseum.ca/sgc-cms/expositions-exhibitions/danewajich/english/places/montney.php and is used with the permission of the Doig River First Nation.

and their descendants. In 1977, when the Dane-zaa split into the Blueberry River and the Doig River Nations, it was discovered that the mineral rights had been lost in error, and never forfeited; thus in 1978, the bands started action against the Crown. Federal Court in 1988 dismissed their claim, finding that the surface land had been sold at less than its value, but that the claim fell outside the 30-year limitation under B.C.'s *Limitation Act*. The Dane-zaa persisted in seeking justice. In 1995, the Supreme Court of Canada found that the Crown had not fulfilled its obligations when it forgot the nation's mineral rights, and were wrong to have not corrected their error when it was first noticed in 1949. The Court awarded damages for royalties, but only from 6.25 sections at Montney that had not yet been transferred to veterans by 1949, as all transfers before that fell outside the 30-year limitation. In 1997, the Doig River and Blueberry River Nations and the Canadian government reached an out-of-court settlement for $147 million as compensation for the lost royalties from those sections. The Dane-zaa received no compensation for the other 21.75 sections.

Here perhaps is a good place to note one difference in the world-view held by the newcomers. White people, arriving, saw the forest and rivers, the muskeg and skies above, as limitless and as *wilderness*. Indigenous nations such as the Dane-zaa, to my knowledge, did not have a concept called "wilderness." They saw the place where they lived as *land* that had its fragilities and needed protecting and care so that the animals and plants upon which they depended could thrive into the future. Whenever the newcomers' activities encroached further into their land, migrations of animals were affected; the traditional schooling of

---

[22] http://maps.fphlcc.ca/dane-zaa "Dane-zaa Záágé? is part of the Athabaskan language family.... It includes the Navajo language of the American Southwest, Hupa, and many languages of Alaska and Canada. Dane-zaa Záágé? is closely related to languages spoken by neighbouring Athabaskan groups, such as Dene Dháh (South Slavey), Sekani, Tsuut'ina (Sarcee), Dene Sųłiné (Chipewyan), and Dene Zågé' (Kaska). Dane-zaa Záágé? is spoken at Hanás Saahgé? (Doig River), Blueberry, Halfway River, and Prophet River in B.C. as well as at the Boyer River (Rocky Lane) and Child Lake (Eleske) Reserves in Alberta.... Dane-zaa Záágé? was our primary language until our grandparents and parents started to send our children to school in the 1950s. English only became dominant in the 1980s. Because our language is orally based, Dane-zaa Záágé? becomes increasingly endangered as our fluent speakers pass away." http://www.virtualmuseum.ca/sgc-cms/expositions-exhibitions/danewajich/english/project/drfn.php

children was interrupted as their children were taken away into residential schools, and the continuity of their cultural practices was threatened. If they raised subjects of interest to their collective communities, no one of the newcomers would attend to what they were saying, and "the Crown" was certainly not helping. Each single encroachment—logging or seismic road—brought others: wells, pipelines, sport hunters, even white squatters trying to go back to the land.

These two world views, of "wilderness" and of "land," were reconciled by some of the earlier white newcomers, who were few in number at first, and who respected the nations among whom they lived and shared resources, but not by most. When people see the land as limitless, and as "wilderness" that is other to their own presence, it is easy to see this land as holding opportunities for making money, and to think that despoliation won't have long-lasting effects. Indigenous peoples, whose seasonal rounds on their lands varied each year so as not to decimate its resources, and to whom the land was not "other," but part of their network of care, realized that making money from the land risked despoliation.

In telling the story of newcomers to the Peace, such as the Callisons and Grendys, it is important to note the background of continuous human life and use of the land upon which their new story is constructed, and critical to recognize the peoples from whom they learned many things, even as their world-views were different. I know that my mother, Anne's sister, did feel troubled at witnessing the treatment of the Dane-zaa and others by Canadian and local governments; still, like other newcomers, the families of this story did not protest on their behalf. The responsibility was not theirs, it seems: it was that of "the Crown."

It's not possible or fair to tell the Dane-zaa story for them, and readers are strongly encouraged to seek out books such as *The Place Where Happiness Dwells* to inform themselves of the Indigenous perspective on the story of these lands. It is only by viewing these perspectives in a spirit of justice that a future sustainable and fair world will be possible.

First Jobs: Making a Life in the North
John on the railway 1921-1928

After the railway that was to connect the Peace River Country with Eastern Canada and the USA had reached Grande Prairie northwest of Edmonton in 1916, the project came to a standstill. The economics of building railways was fraught: full of stops, starts, and bankruptcies. As well, the demand for steel for the war halted many projects. The Northern Alberta Railway (NAR) line was finally extended 24 km from Grande Prairie to Wembley between 1921 and 1924, inching west and north toward its goal, Fort St. John, the oldest European settlement in B.C. But by 1928, the railhead had only reached Hythe, Alberta, 150 km southwest of Fort St. John.

The Callison boys always helped their father Fred in his endeavours to support the family. The older boys, Lynch and John, set an example for the younger, and all learned to work side by side. The railway's arrival in B.C. was long a dream of Fred's, a dream that had fuelled his immigration, so he did what he could to help make it a reality.

Thus, at the age of twelve, in 1921, John Callison was in charge of a team of four horses pulling a fresno scraper,[22] known as a "fresno," for his father, who held the contract to build the railroad grade to Wembley.

VIGNETTE: What on earth is a *Fresno*?

Before the advent of the Fresno in 1883, those building roads had to lug dirt and rocks on carts then dump the load, while others smoothed the surface. The Fresno had a scoop-shaped bucket four to eight feet wide that scraped the ground, and could pick up soil or fill or gravel, then place it where needed, depending on how its operator manipulated the lever controls. With smaller Fresnos, the operator walked behind the team of horses pulling the blade; as Fresnoes got bigger, there was a seat for the operator. As it moved forward, the Fresno left a wide, smooth surface, ready for adding surface gravel or rails.

The grader and motor scraper are modern versions of the Fresno, and the design of bulldozer blades is derived from it as well. Aside from being motorized instead of pulled by horses, the technology is much the same!

---

[22] The fresno was also key in the construction of the Panama Canal!

Within a year or two, John, barely a teenager, drove a team of sixteen horses pulling a fresno over the newly surveyed line. His steady hand and eye, and innate ability to work with horses, were key in laying the railbed smoothly and safely as far as Hythe, 40 km west of Wembley. To handle a fresno with so many horses working in harness in such close proximity took enormous skill.

John grading between Wembley and Hythe with 16 horses, from *Mountain Trails*.

By 1928, rails and ties had been laid and the finished rail line was open as far as Hythe. In late May the next year, the Grendys family, fresh from Ukrainian lands in the state of Poland, arrived in the Peace River district on that very rail line. It is a curious but happy sensation to think of John's future wife Anne arriving safely in Hythe at the age of seven, to go on to the Grendys homestead, thanks in part to John Callison's skilled labour as a teenager. It would be another fourteen years before their paths in life took them this close again.

The Callison boys and their father, in 1928 after the contracts were completed, headed north of their home at Swan Lake to stake out homesteads newly up for allotment just north of Fort St. John, in the Montney District. Eventually, in the 1940s, John and his brothers packed trains of up to forty horses under contract to the US Army and the USA Public Roads Administration, who were surveying, then refining the first army road that was the Alcan Highway.

"In many ways, John's relationship with and care for animals was one of his real gifts. He was able to train them, work with them, and earn their respect as partners in his work as a trapper, as a packer, and as a rancher/farmer," says the text of a speech (uncredited) found in Anne's archives.

John with his toboggan and sled dogs.

Besides working with his brothers and father on contracts for freighting and building, John ran a trapline with them in the late 1920s in the Tumbler Ridge area, south of the Pouce Coupe prairie. By the early 1930s, when the Crown deemed that traplines be registered, John claimed his own trapline in the area of the Kledo River (later Creek), 45 km northwest of Fort Nelson. Starting in 1928, he also worked at the Murdale family homestead, clearing land by hand for farming. As well, John had occasion to travel with his father and brothers more than once to work Fred's registered mineral claims in the area of Quartz Creek near Dease Lake, a trip by horse and pack train of some weeks. John was certainly capable, and busy from a young age. He just seemed to quietly accumulate knowledge, as if he were his own university. He also was known as a singer, who remembered the words to many songs, and he played the mouth organ, along with some fiddle and ukulele. He could cook well, too, and produce a meal of moose steak, onions, bannock, and tea over a fire in the great outdoors that would please anybody. He was an enthusiast of scrub baseball, played wherever a group happened to gather in an open field, and of card games like cribbage and whist. He and his brothers could call a square dance, and if they were somewhere where there weren't enough women partners, some of the men danced the part of girls. He was a pioneer of chuckwagon racing at Dawson Creek later on. People in the early era of settlement invented their own entertainments, and leisure activities depended on their ingenuity and active contributions, for there was little access to radio, no television, restricted access to mail or books, and no way to go to concerts or festivals.

In 1942, when he was almost 33 years old, John's life in the bush on his Kledo River trapline, and on the farm 480 km south in the Montney Valley, was changed forever by the arrival of the US Corps of Engineers to build the Alaska Highway. But let's not jump so far ahead just yet. We can't have the Alcan or Alaska Highway before we bid our respects to its predecessor, the Old Fort Nelson Trail!

Freighting on the Old Fort Nelson Trail
Outside the Homestead Door

There was a trail from Fort St. John to Fort Nelson before the Alaska Highway, and before the Callison family homesteaded north of Fort St. John in 1928.

The trail was originally a Dane-<u>z</u>aa and perhaps Tsek'ene pack trail through the boreal forest of white spruce, and had existed long before European settlement. It ran north from Fort St. John and Charlie Lake, a meeting place active for thousands of years, to the confluence of the Fort Nelson and Muskwa Rivers, another historic staying place, which traders dubbed Fort Nelson, and which local Dene Tha' people knew as *Tthek'eneh Kúe*. There was no other highway, and certainly no train or bus between these places! Near Murdale and Montney, north of Fort St. John, lay places sacred to the dreamers of the Dane-<u>z</u>aa, and the old trail enabled people to travel between various sites on their traditional territories. For many years, especially until the late 1940s when Dane-<u>z</u>aa reserve lands were relocated further north at what today are the Blueberry River, Doig River, and Beatton River reserves,[23] settlers in the Montney Valley such as Anne and John Callison had many day to day interactions with Dane-<u>z</u>aa whom they knew simply as neighbours. John gave work to Indigenous men at haying and harvest time, and was even known to have bailed some unfortunates out of jail in Fort St. John after they'd been found on the wrong side of the rules, and bring them home. Anne remembers John sitting these fellows down in the kitchen at Murdale and asking her to make them coffee, or let them bunk down to sleep, before they all headed out to work stooking or haying or fencing.[24]

The Old Fort Nelson Trail was a wider trail than the old foot or

---

[23] http://calverley.ca/article/01-125-the-st-john-reserve-agricultural-settlement/
[24] At a gathering in February 2018 near Murdale, people said to me that Dane-<u>z</u>aa people returned to the hills of the Montney valley on summer rounds even in the 1960s, camping and meeting where it was hilly or still treed, and not under cultivation. "It was usual to see them." In earlier days of settlement, then, when the populations of Indigenous and white were more in balance and development was still minimal, there was more of a sense of shared inhabitation.

pack horse trail, and was cut in the winter of 1928 in three months by a team of thirty-five men, to make room for horse-drawn wagons, so as to meet the rising demand for the freighting of goods over the 485 km (300 miles) between Fort St. John and Fort Nelson. They slashed trees and cleared a roadbed across watercourses, swamp, and low wetland. The land was so wet and rough that the resulting trail was only passable for teams of horses during the months it was frozen, which made transport even more challenging. Until the late 1930s, the trail was used in summer only on foot with pack dogs, or with strings of pack horses.

A round trip on the Trail from Fort St. John to Fort Nelson and back took about a month. Drovers and freighters made camp whenever they needed to rest their horses, and took turns breaking trail in snowstorms, pulling each other's stuck gear out of drifts and mud and water. They slept on their wagons, or in the closed wagon known as the "caboose" that brought up the rear and held a stove, benches, and other amenities, though it too was piled high with freight! In temperatures that often plunged to 45°C below zero, blankets would freeze stiff on the steaming horses, even as they were pulling hard. The freight wagons were accompanied by many wagons of hay for the horses. Lynch Callison was among the early freighters, ancestors of the truck drivers of today. In fact, when he was naturalized as a Canadian citizen in December 1936, his profession was listed as "freighter" (and his home as Rose Prairie, in the north of the Montney).

Lynch Callison's caboose, freighting on the Old Fort Nelson Trail.

The Old Fort Nelson Trail served newcomers well; it was truly the forerunner of the Alaska Highway. Its presence fed other enterprises: the first settlers' store was opened in Montney by Joe Clarke and Clay Martin, who had their start as storekeepers by bringing supplies to the men who were cutting the Trail. Martin was also a partner in the first sawmill in the Montney Valley, opened in 1928, to provide milled boards to settlers for building barns and houses, saving them the sweaty labour of whipsawing logs by hand to make boards. In 1929, the first school opened at Holdup, another early name for Murdale (in honour of a famed heist there).[25]

So the settler population of the area grew slowly; for over a decade, incoming homesteaders settled further north along the trail, proved up their land, worked on traplines near the mountains in the winter, and created businesses freighting supplies, selling services, and serving their fellow settlers' needs. The decade of the thirties brought the difficulties of the Great Depression everywhere, but in the North Peace, those in both settler and Indigenous communities were quite used to surviving on the resources of the land on which they lived.

---

[25] Larry Evans. "Looking Back: Rural communities north of Fort St. John." *The Alaska Highway News*, June 17, 2010.

The Peace Country in 1928-29 and onward
The Welcoming Wilds

In 1928-29, the last block of the North Peace District had been opened up to homesteaders for settlement and, as Anne wrote, "the hungry land settlers, those hardy souls, came from all over Europe and the States and Canada."[26] Fred Callison and his children John, Lynch, Pat, Lash, and Norma came up from their second homestead near Dawson Creek (following that at Swan Lake) to stake claims on four adjoining quarter sections in the Montney Valley, along the beautiful meanders of Montney Creek, just west of and adjoining the Old Fort Nelson Trail. They worked together in the years that followed to clear the land and "prove up" their holdings, cultivating the new fields with wheat and barley, and with hay and oats for horses. A substantial family home was built of logs on one quarter section, for there was wood close by, cut by axe or handsaw from tall straight trees and dragged out of the forest with horses. Daisy Callison said: "Dad was a wizard with the broad axe. He also did a great job of dovetailing the corners. Shakes were split for the roof. The only materials purchased for the house were glass for windows and nails for the floors and window frames."[27] After the house was built, the family moved there in a wagon with the back covered. Soon enough, a barn was constructed, and, across the creek at a safe distance from other buildings, a blacksmith shop, with a forge for making metal fittings, and shoes for horses.

Fred had settled at the headwaters of Montney Creek as he knew that there were several springs with year-round mineral water there. To him, this was good land that would provide well for his family for generations to come. His early experience in North Dakota with droughts had made him very attentive to water. He loved the valley and its hills and creeks, trees and springs. It was good moose and deer habitat as well. Montney Creek meandered through the property and there were copious springs in the nearby hillside. Father and sons

---

[26] from a typescript of a text in Anne's archives.

[27] Daisy Callison. *Mountain Trails: A Prospecting Expedition from the Diary of a 16-year-old Girl, 1935*. Castlegar, BC: Havdale, 2004, 5.

47

cleared the land with pick and shovel, and ploughed with horses, putting in hard work and long hours. Aside from farming, they also trapped, and hunted for meat (moose, primarily)—doing whatever they could do to make a living.

The Old Fort Nelson Trail passed pretty much in front of Fred Callison's log home. This is probably why, in 1930, when Murdale—the village that encompassed this area of the Montney Valley—obtained a post office, it was run first by Mrs. Fred Callison, out of the front room of their house. After several years, the post office was moved to another farm, and until 1952, you could still send letters to Murdale, BC. Now, Murdale residents get their mail at Montney.

June 18, 1933 – Callison's Murdale Post Office. Back, Left to Right, Charlie Brant, Doris Callison, Harold Rodger, Faith Parker, Lynch Callison, John Callison. Front, Winnie Parker, Lash Callison, Mrs. Fred Callison, child -Marvin Batchler, after a long walk. Charlie, Harold, John and Lash Callison had left Fort Nelson on June 1 and walked to Murdale, arriving June 17. High water made crossing creeks and rivers by rafts for a total of 14 raft crossings.

Photo from Callison family papers, with newspaper caption. Taken outside the Callison house on the homestead, the photo's caption gives an idea of the difficulty of travel in those days!

Down at the meandering creek, there was water, and beaver. There may have been other fish there at one time, but today there are just suckers living on its muddy bottom.

About the house, Anne Callison says: "When we were up north at the river (at the trapline on the Kledo River, 480 km away), we never locked the doors to our house. People didn't lock their doors, then, just in case someone passing through needed a dry place to sleep, and a place to cook a meal."[28] The first settlers, by all accounts, were honorable, as were Indigenous people, and everyone had confidence that even if someone entered a house, they would leave it as it had been found. "That's the way everybody lived," said Anne.

During the survey of the BC Railway extension from Fort St. John to Fort Nelson in the 1960s, which followed the Old Trail across the land, rail surveyors were the ones using the Callison house, while Anne and John were living in Dawson Creek. During this time, there was not the same care with fire and flame as when the blacksmith shop had been first built. In a tragic event for the Callison family, their historic home burned down. No responsibility was ever determined, but Anne felt it was linked to smoking (in those days, more than half of adults smoked), or perhaps to someone building a fire outside the stove, on the floor.

In a later incident, the barn burnt. No one was found responsible then either, but it was a second devastating loss for the Callison family. Neither structure was ever rebuilt, as such, and for some decades there was no home at the old Montney homestead. In the early 1970s, Bill Moure, Anne's sister Mary's young son from Calgary, spent two summers with Anne and John, learning life on the land and farming. Bill remembers John Callison wanting to "work up" some fields on the Murdale homestead. "I'd like to get this field looking really good here," he told Bill when they arrived together from Dawson Creek. Though in his 60s, John still took pride in his farm and wanted it to look well-tilled, even if it took strenuous labour. The homestead by then was easily accessible on a network of well-maintained rural gravel roads, and they fitted out an old cabin to live in, on the other side of the road from where the house and barn had once been. Bill remembers that there

---

28 Melanie Robinson, "Callison Family a part of history in the Northeast," *Northeast News*, Fort St. John, May 2, 2007, 28.

were no structures then on the original homestead. But it was a cherished locale, near the main spring.

A charcoal drawing by Daisy Callison, and one of her paintings, serve to remind the Callison family of the home that once stood there:

Old Callison Homestead

John Callison and his brothers had intimate knowledge of the Montney region by the time the family settled there. Their brother Lynch worked in the 1930s and 1940s hauling freight up to Fort Nelson, and John and other brothers worked for him, moving trains of horse-drawn freight wagons between Dawson Creek, Fort St John, and Fort Nelson. The round trip in those days took about a month, and was only viable when the ground was frozen. John and Lynch, with Lash (a surveyor in the summer), also worked in the winter on registered traplines in the area west of Fort Nelson.

Even for the resourceful Callison family, times were hard in the Depression years of the 1930s. The family ran up $700 in credit at Tucker's Store in Montney Corners. Anne says, "Fur was the only place to make a living so John went to Fort Nelson to trap and pay the debts."

With their father Fred, they also ranged far and wide prospecting for minerals and gold, when claims were opened on Crown land. These claims, just like homesteads, had to be worked to be maintained, and thus in the summer, with hay seeded and traplines put aside till the winter, they would travel together long distances to check their claims and survey trails over the mountains. The tale of one such adventure in 1935 was recorded by John's sister Daisy, the artist. Her diary is the basis for *Mountain Trails: A Prospecting Expedition from the Diary of a 16 year old Girl, 1935*, self-published in 2004. Many of the early photos here come from Daisy's book.

Callison dog teams heading out from Weasel City to trap, early 1940s.

In the late spring of 1942, the Callison brothers came down into Fort Nelson from beaver trapping to sell their furs at George's Trading Post. They found a scene busy with US soldiers, and road equipment, tent encampments, and more. John, Dennis, Lash, and Lynch were all quickly hired as guides and horse packers to help guide US Army highway surveyors through the bush.

By May 1942, then, John was heading from Fort Nelson toward Watson Lake, guiding the surveyors of the US 648th Engineer Topographic Batallion, who blazed the way for the bulldozers of the 35th Engineers,[29] working by dogteam until spring thaw took hold, and with

---

[29] "However, no one knew for certain whether the road could be built, much less what specific route it might follow. Of greatest concern was a proposed stretch of territory between Fort Nelson, BC, and Watson Lake, Yukon Territory, since little or no survey data existed for that area." Shawn Umbrell, *First on the Line: The 35th Engineer Battalion in World War Two and the Evolution of a High-Performance Combat Unit*. Master's thesis, U of Toledo, 1998, 52-53, online.

strings of pack horses thereafter. Both were safe means of transportation in the irregular territory, which was full of muskeg, trees, rivers, frozen ground and quagmires of mud once unfrozen. The only other mode of transport at the time was walking, with pack dogs carrying small loads.

4 Brothers Lead Americans In Alaska Road Route Quest

Will Take Men Into Uncharted Areas of Northwest

TRAPPERS, PIONEERS

By Don Menzies
(Edmonton Journal Staff Reporter)

DAWSON CREEK, B.C., March 20.—When the saga of the Alaska highway is written, four brothers, all trappers, traders and ranchers, will figure prominently.

The brothers will take U.S. engineer units by dog team into the uncharted areas between Fort St. John and Fort Nelson, and Fort Nelson and Watson Lake, to blaze the trail which eventually will become the North American continent's most vital road.

They are Elisha, John, Dennis and Lynch Collison, who operate a ranch north of Fort St. John and trading posts in the north, including Fort Nelson.

These brothers have traveled over vast areas in the north by dog team and pack horse and have an excellent knowledge of Indian trails. They even have blazed trails themselves.

The brothers will take American survey parties into areas which will be selected from reconnaissance planes as logical routes for the highway. The survey parties will study ground conditions, return and make their findings known, then start out to blaze the Alaska highway.

This clipping from the Edmonton Journal, 1942, was in reference to the part my brothers played in the building of the Alaska Highway.

Edmonton Journal article, March 20, 1942.

52

Many history books mention the local men, trappers and wranglers of horses who helped the Americans, calling them "Bushmen" and "Natives." These books tend to describe the region as empty and desolate forest, and the people as primitive. But it wasn't so; the Callisons and others like them, and the Dane-ẕaa, Tsek'ene, Dene Tha', Métis, and Cree people in the area used every modern convenience that they could. It's just that with only about 5000 people in the whole Peace region before the coming of the US forces (only 1000 or so in the immediate area of Fort Nelson), it was not highly populated. But people were there. When history books mention the guides who steered the US Engineers and roadbuilders through bush and mountains, away from the muskeg, it's important to note that the young Callison men were among them, helping blaze the trail for the road along with Indigenous guides based in and near Fort Nelson, such as Charlie McDonald and Archie Gairdner.

Of all the brothers, it was John who never left the family homestead for greener pastures; to him, Murdale was as green as a pasture gets. As Fred Callison's other sons moved away and took up other careers, John bought up their land, and continued to live and farm at Murdale.

In early years of clearing and planting in the 1930s and 1940s, John had continued to live on his trapline in the winter, moving to the homestead to farm in the summer. That was the rhythm of his life when he met the young Anne Grendys in the early spring of 1943 at Arthur and Lodema George's bustling store, the centre of Old Fort Nelson, when he came in with his load of furs from his trapline on the Kledo River.

Before we tell that story, let's catch up with Anne Callison back in the South Peace, at the Grendys farm on top of Saskatoon Mountain!

A Woman Heading Out to Work
Anne heads to High Prairie in 1941

After growing up on Saskatoon Mountain in the 1930s, in the South Peace several kilometres north of the hamlet of Huallen, Alberta, Anne Grendys reached the end of the Great Depression with a desire to see more of the world. She had left school early to look after her mother and help on the farm, and learned a lot, but the wider world was calling to her. She was a determined woman, with a taste for adventure.

As she had proven skills in caring for the sick, she found a job in High Prairie, Alberta, in the spring of 1941, working as a nurses' aide at the Providence Hospital, run—as were many small-town Alberta hospitals—by the Roman Catholic nursing order of the Sisters of Charity of Providence from Montreal, who had arrived in 1937 to take over a small hospital started by a doctor. Their mission was to bring medical assistance to those who needed it. In 1940, they commissioned construction of a new wing as the hospital at High Prairie was already too busy. When it opened in 1941, the new wing included residential facilities for staff, as more staff were needed. Anne had already had experience in her own family, nursing her mother after an operation. She knew it was something she was able to handle, and it would bring her new experiences in a real town, and urban independence. It would satisfy her spirited craving for adventure.

Anne's personal photo album holds two postcards of the hospital and the town, and several photos of herself with her friend Gertie. A few pages later, there is a photo of her marked "Myself, May 1941." Anne would have been 19 years old. There are other photos of her, mostly taken in May of 1941, with the hospital in the background, featuring Anne and Gertie, Sister Frances, Sister Alphonse, Sister Rose, Noella Moran, Katherine Dayner, among others. The hospital staff included lay Registered Nurses as well as the nursing nuns, and nurses' aides.

Sister Frances, Anne, Sister Rose, Gertie   Anne and Gerty

Anne also worked closer to home before and after she lived in High Prairie, at jobs that ranged from live-in mother's helper on another farm to cooking for groups during a summer at the McNaught Homestead south of Beaverlodge (once home of Euphemia McNaught, a noted painter of landscapes in the area, taught by a member of the Group of Seven).[30]

Another wonderful selection of photos in Anne's album depict her at the farm on Saskatoon Mountain in early 1942, many outside in the snow. In quite a few photos from that spring, she is keeping company

---

[30]http://hermis.alberta.ca/ARHP/Details.aspx?DeptID=1&ObjectID=4665-0873

with a dashing fellow named Dave Bauman, brother of Anne's friend Mary. Dave was Anne's boyfriend at this point in time. "We were quite serious," she said, "and were engaged to be married. But," Anne says, looking mischievous as if remembering a happy dream, but speaking with gravity, "I met someone else, and I jilted Dave." That someone, she says, was John Callison, in 1943.

Other photos in Anne's album show neighbours Taras and Mary Nychka[31] in 1937, members of the nearby homesteading family who had, years earlier, housed the Mountain Trail School teacher, to the consternation of the more "English" members of the school district, who wrote the deputy minister of Education in the mid-1930s to complain and ask for his intervention to have the teacher boarded with an English family! The nerve! The deputy minister replied that it was up to the teacher where she wanted to board, and rightly so. This tale makes many a person of Ukrainian heritage snicker, for of course the teacher would want to stay in a Ukrainian house: oh the great cooking![32]

There are earlier photos as well, of Anne with her mother's energetic border collie Sport in July of 1941, of her brother Joe with "Pete," both in army uniform that same year in Grande Prairie. There is a photo of two women—Anne and her friend Evelyn Tolway—playing shy in a clutch of small aspens; one of Evelyn with a bicycle, aspens and snow in the background; and one of Anne, her sister Mary, and Evelyn in some bushes near a house.

Women often vanish in history, because they changed their names when they married in those days, and often left their home communities to live far from their families. Evelyn Tolway, the girl with the bicycle, did leave a trace. She was the third child of seven of Frank (died June 29, 1970, age 91) and Eva Tolway, who immigrated from Poland (from a town in a district NE of Lviv, thus in today's Ukraine) in 1927 with their first five children and homesteaded near Hythe. Evelyn was born in 1925, and later married a John Packolyk and lived further south in Alberta, near Leduc, which could indicate that her husband worked in the oil and gas industry. She died in 2000, and her husband in 2008.

---

[31] Taras Nychka died in 1974; his wife Mary (nee Maiko) died in Beaverlodge AB, on August 6, 2003, age 85.

[32] This story comes from my research in the South Peace Archives in Grande Prairie, in the schools file for Mountain Trail School, conducted in 2008 or 2009.

There is a John Packolyk who as of 2017 was still working in the oil industry in Leduc; perhaps they are related![33]

Anne Callison and Dave Bauman, 1942. Dave was a young farmer, famed for his skill with horses. It seems Anne admired the horsemen! There are numerous photos in her albums, too small and blurry to reproduce well, showing Dave's exploits back in those days, both rodeoing and ploughing. Here they are at the Bauman family sawmill.

---

[33]http://southpeacearchives.org/holdings-2/finding-aids/fonds-642-adam-tolway-fonds/ "Frank's two brothers (Anton, born Skrycholowa Poland, died Hythe AB, July 16, 1987, age 93, and John) also made the journey and settled in the area." "Frank and Eva's children Ludwig, Ada, Evelyn, Adam (b. July 12, 1922 Poland, d. Sept 22, 1944 in action with the Calgary Highlanders, while clearing the port of Antwerp, Belgium, possibly in the famed action of the Highlanders at Albert Canal http://www.calgaryhighlanders.com/history/highlanders/personalities/crockett.htm) and Mary immigrated with their parents; siblings Walter and Edmund were born in Canada. Mary died in 1929 and was buried in the Hay Cemetery along with some of her Tolway cousins who had all contracted scarlet fever."

Joe and Anne, hand in hand with Dave, all dressed up. Note Dave's fancy-cut vest and snazzy leather jacket (this was before James Dean!), and Joe's dress uniform. Of course, Sport the dog puts in an appearance, sniffing Anne's shoe!

Anne, Evelyn, and Mary outside the east wall of "the new house," 1942. "The car is not ours. I don't travel in it," Anne wrote on the back; "as I'd have to push sometimes!"

Sisters Vella and Kathleen Carter with Anne's brother Joe in his army uniform at the Carter farm west of Sexsmith, AB. Joe dated both sisters, apparently, having met them while working as a farmhand for their father, John Roy Carter. After the war, Joe married Kathy in a double wedding with Vella and her new husband. Joe and Kathy then took over the farm on the Grendys homestead from the elder Grendys, as Tom and Nelly moved toward a well-deserved retirement.

Earlier in life, around 1933: a moment of respite and music with a neighbour accordionist. Tom Grendys is at front right, and Mary and Anne Grendys stand behind the men, against the wall of the house.

Mary Kachaluba's Wedding, 1942, with Anne and Mary Grendys as bridesmaids (flowers in hair), and their mother Nelly (centre, back row). Mary K was greatly admired; after Anne left school, Mary K continued to go with Mary G, who always said Mary K was smarter: "she never had to study! She aced every test!" After marriage, Mary Kachaluba is one of those women whose trace is hard to follow.

Evelyn Tolway and bicycle; Anne on her horse Fanny.

Anne, Mary, and Sport the dog, Saskatoon Mountain homestead, 1939.

Anastasia, Mary, Anne, and the cows, 1939, on Saskatoon Mountain, taken when the snow was melting, probably in April of that year.

All dressed up at the Grendys homestead, March and April 1939. To the left, Joe behind with his arms around Anne and Mary, with Nelly in front. To the right, Anne and Mary, two sisters in their teenage years.

Dave Bauman and his father Jim (Simeon) Bauman (or Jim McLauchlan—Anne could only say it was "Jim") ploughing with two teams of six horses, at their homestead, spring 1942.

Butchering a pig, 1942: Jim and Dave Bauman, with Tom Grendys in the background. Look out for that handsaw! The barn they is made of peeled logs chinked with cement, but the sliding door is newer: it's made of finely milled boards, possibly from the Bauman mill.

Anne with Adam. "Not the one I am really going out with," she wrote on the back. "He looks old here but he's only 18." Anne admits to having lots of boyfriends before going steady with Dave in 1942.

Taras and Marg Nychka and their friends... a stylish skating party! Around 1940.

Lovely Anne Grendys, near Huallen AB, summer 1942, 20 years old. People might have ploughed with horses and butchered with hand saws, but there was no shortage of high fashion at the time! Women were talented at sewing and restyling clothes.

Alcan Highway
Muskeg and Muck and American Soldiers

The first Alcan—later Alaska—Highway was built in eight months and twelve days in 1942, while Anne Grendys was back on the family farm north of Huallen, Alberta. The new highway was cut across boreal forest and muskeg, lakes and creeks, gulleys and mountains using bulldozers and hand labour, right through the North Peace district of British Columbia, to link Alaska to the rest of the continental USA in the middle of the Second World War when the USA was under threat from Japan.

The North Peace was a forested land of animals and fish, hunters and trappers—mostly Indigenous with a scattering of white people, living in much the same way as people did in the 18th and 19th century. Anyone using the land or travelling through it knew how to map, track, read signs of animals and waters, muskeg and mountain, wind and mosses, and hunt, or they hired people who did. They had to be able to pack the supplies they needed, and to use the resources of the land judiciously to ensure continuity of life: the timber and its animals, the grasses and waters, the places of dreams and ancestors. The Dane-zaa people had adopted horses, and became skilled wranglers; they developed their own way of riding and tack to fit their needs as hunters.

The newcomers who had made incursions on the rich soils of the rolling lands north and east of Fort St. John to farm following the signing of Treaty 8, especially after the railway drew closer, were a much more recent phenomenon. Even they trapped and hunted part of the year to survive, penetrating the traditional territories on which the First Nations had the right to hunt and trap forever, causing much worry and consternation even before the highway. The highway changed much, but the change in mentalities that came with "Crown land" was already in process. What had long been a land of rivers and wildlife, and peoples caring for the land according to ancient custom even as they adopted new ways, very far away from the brutal wars of the so-called "civilized world," would become open to that civilization. To the newcomers, lands not yet exploited by machines for the purpose of the accumulation of wealth were known as "wilderness." The rest became "opened to civilization." To Indigenous peoples, there was no binary of wilderness and civilization; the bush, prairies, rivers, and mountains were their land, and it nurtured them, harboured their traditions and dreams, protected animals and humans alike, and gave rise to their economy and civil society, and would provide for their future.

The massive engineering work of building the Alcan (**Al**aska-**Can**ada) Highway—one of two great US military engineering works of the 20th century, along with the Panama Canal—was to alter lives in ways that at the time would have been unimaginable. Increased urban and rural settlement, resource exploitation, big-game trophy hunting, sport fishing, and tourism followed the highway, and ushered in settler cultures that would thrive more on accumulation of goods than on ties with extended families, ancestors, seasons, and the natural world.

As B.C.'s population grew, the area would also be soon harnessed for hydro-electric power, with dams built on the Peace River, flooding its low and rich valleys and those of its main tributaries from the Rocky Mountains. Dams brought jobs, though mostly to newcomers, as Indigenous men were little involved in the construction apart from working as guides and swampers. Indigenous women, in the first era of highway and dam building, were hired to do laundry, make and mend parkas and mukluks, moccasins, purses, and souvenirs, and they worked occasionally in canteens or offices. The construction altered wildlife migration, climate, sacred sites, and landforms. As farmers, ranchers, and resource developers moved in, Indigenous peoples would gradually lose use of traditional land as reserves were moved and altered, and access to their hunting territories was restricted by private land ownership. As much as they could, the Indigenous peoples retreated to where the newcomers had not yet made incursions, but they also became part of the new economy, especially as traditional life was made more precarious. Diseases arrived as well with the construction crews (just as smallpox arrived with the fur trade), exposing people to measles, influenza, dysentery, mumps, whooping cough, and meningitis. Death rates in Indigenous groups soared after construction of the highway.

Highways also disrupted patterns of animal movement. Residential schools loomed as an increasing menace, with government payments such as family allowance withheld to anyone reluctant to send their children. In sum, the glorious new highway, it is only fair to note, frayed the autonomy of the peoples whose history was tied to that of the land,

and put pressures on Indigenous economies, and on family and social structures, in ways that continue to affect their descendants today.[32]

By the time the US Army Corps of Engineers arrived in March 1942 in the Peace Country, three of the white trappers who worked winter traplines in the area of Fort Nelson were members of the Callison family. John and his brother Lash and cousin George Lynch all had traplines along the winding Kledo River and in the two watersheds to the northwest, 45 km west of Fort Nelson. They had built winter cabins years before, and kept their dog teams and horses close to each other, at a point where their lines met up. Other trappers also lived there, such as Henry Courvoisier and Bert Sheffield, later infamous as partners in a huge fur robbery, though Henry was also fabled as a violinist, who carried his violin on the trapline. The low flood plain where they all lived, at the confluence of the Kledo and the Muskwa River, was wryly named "Weasel City."

Their quiet but rugged life of subsistence off the land, according to the traditions of the fur trade and even older customs, was to be suddenly altered in 1942. As was the life of all those who served the fur trade, as buyers and bunkers of trappers, among whom were Arthur and Lodema George with their stopping place and store in Old Fort Nelson. The tsunamis of change would also alter the life of Anne Grendys of Huallen, Alberta.

A land route linking Alaska to the forty-eight southern United States was not a new idea; it had been contemplated back in the 1920s, and the Canadian and BC governments were involved in discussions, but the challenges were many, and the huge resources only committed after the United States was attacked by Japan in World War II, at Pearl Harbor in Hawaii on December 7, 1941. The highway then was suddenly seen as a vital link allowing expansion and maintenance of a line of northern airports through Canada that were crucial to defense of Pacific sea lanes from the enemy, and that provided succour from the east to and from Russia, then an ally.

Seven US regiments from the Army Corps of Engineers were sent north to Dawson Creek in March 1942 ("the trains just kept coming and coming," said the locals) to build the "pioneer road" that was the first trace of the Alaska Highway.

---

[32] See http://ouralaskahighway.com/?page_id=1011, the "First Nations" tab.

Before Leaving the States

Weather (What to Expect)

The winters here are long and cold with occasional icy conditions hampering private travel. Snowfall usually begins in September and lasts until early May. Actually the average frost free period lasts just ninety days. The temperature has been known to fall as low as fifty degrees below zero, and remain there for a week or more; however, this is an unusual situation. The monthly average of daily mean temperature for the coldest month (January) registers at six above zero and the annual at thirty-five. The summers are beautiful: comfortably warm in the daytime and cool at night. This is slightly marred by an abundance of rainfall in June and July and a bumper crop of mosquitoes. Also, in the spring and summer, as a result of spring thaw and summer rains, much mud is to be found making driving on unpaved roads difficult and dangerous. If this reads like the dark side, it is because we want you to be prepared. Bring your snow shoes, raincoat and mosquito repellent.

From US Army handbook for Communications units sent to work on the highway (temperatures in Fahrenheit).

By the end of June, 6000 soldiers were at work, stationed at three staging points—Fort St. John, Fort Nelson, and Whitehorse—and working forward and backward from there. The number of troops later rose to nearly 11,000, and there were hundreds of trainloads of bulldozers, tents, graders, and endless other supplies.

As US Brigadier-General William Hoge, who led the project, later said, "We were under orders to push the pioneer road through to Fairbanks in nine months. We couldn't wait for surveys.... We had no maps. We used maps I found in old National Geographic magazines. We had no soil surveys and only found out about permafrost when it was too late. After we cut down the trees and stripped the overburden, trucks and caterpillars sank into the muck till they were out of sight. I thought they'd end up in China."[33]

After a route was mapped from the air, US Army surveyors were forced to work quickly on the ground, with no geographical knowledge. They made mistakes until they hired local trappers, Indigenous and white, who guided them by dogsled and pack horse to finalize the route. They cut just a trail at first for their own pack trains, flagging it. The bulldozers followed, flattening everything in sight and pushing trees to the side. Because survey and clearing crews worked beyond where trucks

---

[33] Les McLaughlin, "North to Alaska," in *Legion: Canada's Military History*, Sept. 1, 2002. Online.

could venture, they were provisioned by packhorses; they slept in tents and moved forward daily. Following the clearing crews, groups of soldiers built bridges and installed culverts, and they in turn were followed by crews who dug drainage ditches to the side and built up the grade to allow trucks to travel without being mired. Later, the first road was straightened, widened, and gravelled.

In the words of a US administrative officer, reporting in 1943 to his superiors about the first work on the highway in 1942:

> There were mountains everywhere, linked and overladen with illimitable forests. Sprawling rivers, scores of vast swamp areas and a multitude of lakes presented problems seldom encountered in a similar undertaking. Canyon floors were explored by low-flying planes, dangerously guided through jumbled mountains.
>
> A rutted provincial road between Dawson Creek and Fort St. John afforded the only approach to the southern base of operations. A narrow winter road from Fort St. John to Fort Nelson, 216 miles north, provided the only access to the forest itself. From Fort St. John north and west for almost 1,500 miles the wilderness was broken only by dog and pack trails or short stretches of winter road, serviceable only until made impassable by the spring thaw. [...]
>
> The Indian trails could be used only in winter, and the men who followed them were not concerned with muskeg or swamps, since the ground was frozen. The flat swamp areas generally offered easier access to a given destination than a route through rougher country. The so-called winter roads in the North are useful only when the ground is frozen...
>
> But aerial reconnaissance was only the beginning in fixing the route of the highway. Thereafter, and even while location engineers of the Army and Public Roads Administration were flying almost daily over the general route chosen, foot and dogsled examination of the area to be traversed were still necessary to check conclusions from air reconnaissance. Even then there were problems of grade and curvature to be solved before locations could be determined definitely.[34]

The US Army was segregated in those days; Black soldiers served separately from whites. The Army sent white regiments at first, shamefully lacking confidence in the regiments of Black soldiers whom

---

[34] Theodore A. Huntley. *Construction of the Alaska Highway.* Washington, Sept. 1945, 3-7, condensing a report Huntley had prepared in 1943 for his superiors.

they saw as good for back-breaking toil but not for leading in unmarked territory, and whom they felt would not survive in Canadian cold (who knows why they thought white troops would—since the key is being dressed properly!). Quickly recognizing the magnitude of the task, however, three Black engineering regiments—with white Southern officers—were added in March 1942, arriving in May of that year.

The 95th Engineer Regiment was the first Black regiment to arrive at Dawson Creek in 1942, charged with improving the first road bulldozed the month before from Fort St. John to Fort Nelson, west of the Old Fort Nelson Trail and Charlie Lake. Meanwhile, white troops blazed the road further toward Fort Nelson. By the end of the summer, Black engineering troops were 40% of the labour force. They worked the same jobs, but were segregated in camps away from towns and villages. Their equipment was largely that unwanted by white regiments, who could boast of using the world's largest tractor, the D-8 Diesel, 7.5 feet high, 15 feet long, 9 feet wide. The D-8s pushed forward four to five abreast to knock down the trees. Black troops had D-4 cats and smaller graders, and often made do with shovels, picks, handsaws, and back muscles. The winter of 1942-43 sapped morale in record-breaking cold, with temperatures plunging to minus 60-70 degrees Fahrenheit (-50-56°C.) In that cold, Army issue clothing was utterly inadequate, and military crews, Black and white, were unable to work. Civilian contractors kept their personnel better supplied, so they worked in almost all weather.[35]

The racist attitudes that gave rise to this situation have often been described.[36] Despite them, Black troops accomplished so much, so

---

[35] from "Black Regiments," *The Alaska Highway: A Yukon Perspective*, Yukon Archives, 1992. www.alaskahighwayarchives.ca/en/resources/credits.php

[36] Barry Broadfoot, *Six War Years 1939-1945*, U Toronto Press, 1970, 217: "In those days, they were segregated and they did all the rough work. Some drove trucks and tractors, but they also did an awful lot of pure back-breaking bull labour, axe work and pick and shovel. And they hated it. At the beginning they were poorly housed; they just had tents. And it was cold. You'd see them standing around huge fires they'd made from the lumber to be used for construction, buildings, cribbing, bridge timbers. They burned everything; it didn't matter. They were poorly clothed; they didn't have Arctic-type clothing or decent boots. They had no recreation; there was nothing fun for them to do. They were segregated in a land of nowhere and they were miserable." Broadfoot may have been overstating the misery, as the camaraderie and resilient problem-solving attitudes of the troops alleviated misery somewhat. But many later said: "We had never seen country or cold like it. We thought we'd never again go home."

quickly, and so well that they elicited only admiration. Their successes and endurance had a landmark effect: they gave rise to the desegregation of American armed forces after World War Two, as the excuses for keeping the troops separate were exposed as a sham. This change helped put pressure on civil society for desegregation as well, though it took the 1960s Civil Rights movement protests to really enact change. Acknowledgement of the Black regiments came only slowly: in the 1990s, they were finally honoured for their role in building the Highway.

All the US engineer regiments worked twelve to fourteen hour days as loggers, catskinners, sawmillers of wood for bridges and corduroy, organizers of camps where they lived in six-man pyramid tents for a week at a time before moving forward. All found it cold in these tents coated with sheets of icicles, and shivered in layers of military clothing.

A caterpillar tractor widens the bed of the Alaska Highway, 1942.

When spring and summer came, troops were eaten alive by swarms of mosquitoes and black flies, gnats, and no-see-ums—their Army had sent all the bug repellent to Europe!

This was the scene that met John Callison and his brothers and cousin when they came out from their traplines on the Kledo in the spring of 1942, arriving with their pelts to a Fort Nelson full of soldiers. They then witnessed, in disbelief, what happened at spring break-up, when US Army engineers, ignorant of muskeg and permafrost, removed ground cover to create the roadbed. With its protective insulation gone, the permafrost below simply melted, and road and machines sank and vanished into the endless muck and water known as "gumbo."

The engineers resorted to filling the roadbed with logs (corduroy) before it could thaw, piling branches on top to insulate before adding earth fill and gravel. With the fight against melting permafrost, their aim of building a 36 foot wide road was abandoned. The first road was at times only 12-18 feet wide—barely possible for truck convoys to pass.

Building Corduroy Road. Note the hats with mosquito nets.

John and Dennis Callison were hired to help direct US surveyors north from Fort Nelson to Summit Lake, to blaze routes that avoided the valley muskeg where possible. Where the road crossed their traplines at the Kledo River, the 35th Engineers built several structures as a construction base. John later helped surveyors go onward from Summit Lake up to Watson Lake. When the pioneer road was turned over to the US Public Roads Administration for widening in 1942 and 1943, John Callison was among the civilian contractors. "He had three pack strings of horses working for him on different areas of the highway for a year or two," says Anne. "He then packed 35 to 40 of his own horses for the P.R.A." His job was to move the camps of construction workers each week, at different points on the road from Fort St. John to the Sikanni Chief River. Other trappers worked elsewhere packing horses. The Callisons' experience with surveying and building the railway in the 1920s in Alberta as teenagers served them well in understanding the needs of the Army. The proceeds from one of his pack strings, says Anne, earned John (then 33) his first car, a rare event in those times.

VIGNETTE—Call Those Men Off That Hopeless Job

"When John Callison arrived in Fort Nelson after beavering in the late spring of 1942, he was amazed to see a new townsite bustling above the old, and hundreds of soldiers where, the fall before, there'd been a quiet trading post. He found a group of Black soldiers digging the oozing muskeg, sinking into their own hole, batting mosquitoes and sweating in the chilly sun. He asked them what on earth they thought they were doing, and they said they were removing the crust to build the road. John told them this was useless; they'd never get to the bottom, and they should get out of the hole. They told him they had their orders. John brought them cold water to drink and then went off to find the officer in charge. When he found the fellow and told him his soldiers should be ordered to stop, he was told by a petty officer to mind his own business." As Daisy Callison puts it: "John, always a gentleman, did not like the officer's attitude and quietly told him not to confuse himself with God Almighty. He would not do a useless dirty job like that himself. If he wanted to destroy any respect the Canadians had for them, just leave those boys in that mud hole! The senior officer, listening in, heard John say they could dig to China and find no bottom to the muskeg, which is like quicksand. He sent the first officer to call the men off their hopeless job immediately. (John said he never met any of those dark boys personally, but he was certainly spoken to in a most friendly manner and got many pats on the back and smiles!) The coloured boys had told John where the Army intended to build the highway, so John told the officers that they were heading right through miles of muskeg and were stupid. John was willing to draw a map for them, not straight but high and crooked, to show them where to build. What they really needed was experienced men with trained horses and dogs to pack them over the trail."[37]

The Army offered John a job, but he needed first to head to Vancouver to sell his furs, then get back to Montney and plant his crops at the homestead. He was never a man to walk away from responsibility, though. Under pressure, and called to be patriotic, he agreed to work with them, and bring his brothers too.

---

[37] from Daisy Callison. *Mountain Trails*, 188. (Though the newspaper said the Callison boys were hired to survey in March, John was still on his trapline then.)

John Callison's pack train while working for the American Army on the Alaska Highway survey in 1942

The highway officially opened at the end of November of 1942, at a ceremony at Soldier's Summit at Historic Mile 1061, in the Yukon. It was -37°F. The highway was still a pioneer road, a "rutted quagmire" only passable in the winter when the muskeg froze. In 1943, US Army regiments were gradually withdrawn and the road turned over to civilian contractors for the US Public Roads Administration. US Army Signal Corps regiments arrived in spring of 1943 to handle communications and logistics for the army truck convoys that travelled along the Pioneer Road supplying airports and camps, as the road was still being improved, widened, and rerouted. There was still plenty of US Army presence.

In April 1943, Edwin Gutherlet, a 21 year old sergeant in the 843rd Signal Service Battalion, was one of the first US signalling troops to arrive on the pioneer road. He wrote home[38] about heading north from Dawson Creek and vividly described the fabulous new Alcan Highway: "We now found ourselves on nothing but a trail through the woods, melting snow and mud were everywhere. We travelled in 1st and 2nd gears and four-wheel drive, and used chains on all wheels. In many cases the running boards barely cleared the top of the mud. At one point we were not certain where the road ran. Anywhere you looked there were trees, standing water, and mud. One man sat on the flat hood of the

---

[38] Eric Jensen. *Forever and a Day: The World War II Odyssey of an American Family*. Denver, CO: Outskirts Press, 2009, 95-96.

Reconnaissance Car with a pole, trying to feel where the road might be found. After driving over seven hundred miles through so much swamp and lowlands, we came to the Continental Divide. We came down a steep grade, went across a bridge over Seagull Creek, and stopped a short distance later at our new home."[39]

By 1943, locals' lives in Dawson Creek, Fort St. John, Fort Nelson, and all up and down the road, were thoroughly disrupted! Among them were Arthur and Lodema George, who ran a bustling store and café they had started in 1938 in a tent in Old Fort Nelson, before building a shared home and store space, with bedroom and kitchen at the back of the store, and bunkroom on the top floor to rent beds to trappers coming in to sell their furs. The service counter ran along one wall, and in back was a large table where they served meals family-style to up to 14 people at a time. The clear part of the floor in front was used to hold dances and gatherings, as well as to sort and grade piles of furs. The Georges also ran the Post Office. Before the US army came to town, Old Fort Nelson was a sleepy village with a Game Warden office, a BC Police post, a Hudson's Bay trading post, the George's stopping place and café, a Catholic mission and church known as "Our Lady of the Snows," and log cabins and teepees that were home to Dane-zaa and Cree families, fur traders, some white trappers, and Catholic priests.

In 1942, said Lodema George, "the Americans took over. They had money and spent millions. We had the only place that anyone could go for a meal; after the soldiers heard there was a café nearby, they just about mobbed us."[40] They were all sick of army rations, and were frozen cold in the winter, and had few or no recreational facilities. George's Store and Café became a place of recreation, a place to get warm, to meet up and have pie and coffee, dig into a home-cooked meal, or just stand over the woodstove. In summer, Mrs. George grew a large garden out back of the store, so had her own supply of fresh vegetables, and of course there was lots of wild meat, especially moose. Mrs. George's six-foot square post office, which used to get a big bag of mail once a month, suddenly was getting 18-20 bags a day, seven days a week! She was overwhelmed and pleaded with the officer in charge, who told her she didn't have to sort them. He sent soldiers to collect the bags each

---

[39] Today the Swift River Maintenance Camp, and Lodge at km 1136.7, Historical Mile 733.

[40] Gerri F. Young. *The Fort Nelson Story*. Fort Nelson, BC, 1980, 71.

day and bring them to the camp at the airport. Still, for a few hours every day there was no room for furs: the store was top to bottom with mailbags!

The army men were homesick and lovelorn, and came to the store to confide their woes and dreams, visit the young women who worked there, and tell tales of the accidents and the hard work and aches, the boredom and the mosquitoes, and the crazy solutions they found to problems. During the first August and September, in 1942, the Georges served an average of 150 meals a day. Mrs. George also sewed fur collars and pieces, mittens and mukluks, and employed other young women to do sewing as well, making souvenirs, really, because the soldiers were avid to bring home local gifts to their girlfriends and mothers that would show off the particularities of the place where they were stationed. And where else was there to buy gifts made of fur and hide, beautifully lined, embroidered, and beaded? George's Store![41]

By late 1942, Lodema George was desperate for more help for both sewing and cooking, and heard tell of an adventurous young woman in Huallen, Alberta who was a great cook and had no fear of hard work; she might be up for the challenge. This woman was Anne Grendys, and Mrs. George wrote to her in Huallen in November 1942 and offered her a job as a cook. Anne, just about to turn twenty-one, answered favourably and said she'd come in January, 1943.

At that time, the Alcan highway was "open" to military use only. The road was traversed daily by convoys of trucks (pilots flying overhead reported that the highway looked like Broadway, it was so lit up by headlights!) carrying materials and fuel to the airports, and to the bases along the way. Military permission was needed to travel on the road. In Fort Nelson, as spring light started to return in March of 1943, Arthur and Lodema George's cafe and store was still bustling with soldiers, just as the trappers were arriving from their lines to sell their winter catch of furs.

As we conclude our tale of the initial building of the Alcan Highway, let's contrast Sergeant Gutherlet's words regarding the swamps and lowlands that he faced in 1943, the year after the highway was first finished, with Anne Callison's reminiscences of a retirement trip with John, a half-century in the future: "John and I finally made our

---

[41] Gerri F. Young, 77.

first trip as tourists up the Alaska Highway in June 1992, fifty years later. Roads were very good and the scenery still beautiful."

But we're not in the future quite yet! Let's snoop now in Anne Grendys's mail from November, 1942. (Later, we'll go back to see what happened to the Callisons *after* the highway was built, as the story of the road doesn't end here!)

Fort Nelson B.C.   Nov. 16,1942

Dear Miss Gundys;

Your friend Therza Romenoff told me to write
you about coming to Nelson to cook for me.   I have a
trappers boarding house and now there are some soldiers that
come ovre for a meal now and again. The meals are family style
no short orders.

The trappers are all out on their lines now but
will be in during the holidays. We serve pie or doughnuts and
coffee between meals if any comes in.

The last girl I had (Ivy Murray) came last Jan.
and left me Nov. lst ,she is married and living next door, and
now I am doing the work alone but I have to much other work , I am
Postmistress and we have a store and Mr George is a fur buyer ad
and I do the ordering for the store, and sewing when I have time.

Our household consists of two younge men woking
in the store and Mr George and myself.   There is practically no
house work, no rooms except your own and the kitchen and I always help with the washing.   I will pay $50.00 a month and your
fare in and if you stay six months your transportation out. Of
course I would like you to stay the six months as the fare in is
high ,I would have you go to Grand Prarie and fly from there

I wish you would wire me at once collect if you
will come or not , if you come I will make arrangement for you
to come at once. I might add I am 52 years old.

The re are a few soldiers at the air port three
miles from here.   Yours truly, Mrs Arthur George.

The famed letter from Mrs. Lodema George to Miss Anne Grendys in November,
1942. Anne has carried it with her all her life, as it sealed her destiny and gave a
new direction to her life.

80

A Woman's View of the Early Years on the Alcan
by Anne Callison[42]

In November 1942, just about a month before my 21st birthday, I received a letter from Mrs. George, needing help at their family's fur trading post in Fort Nelson. She ran a "trappers' boarding house" and told me that "there are some soldiers that come over for a meal now and then." She would pay $50.00 a month and all expenses.

I wrote back and said that I would take the job but that I could not come until after Christmas. She said that was fine, went ahead and made all my travel arrangements.

On January 2, 1943, I took the train from Beaverlodge, Alberta to Dawson Creek, where I was met by a nurse and taken to St. Joseph's Hospital, where Mrs. George had arranged that I would stay overnight in the nurses' quarters. Come evening, on arrival, there was no room for me! The nuns soon solved that! They gave me a bed in a ward, in the fourth bed, with three patients in the other beds. Another nurse, coming into the ward in the morning, was surprised to see me and wanted to know what was going on! Soon she had me checked out and said it was okay to be there.

To travel the Alaska Highway, I had to have a letter stating where I was going to work, before the United States Government would issue a pass to me. I was assigned to travel with the Highway Superintendent who was taking mail and machine parts in a truck along the Highway. We left around noon; there was not that much daylight in January and it was very cold. Roads were good.

We arrived at night at Mile 295 [at the Sikanni Chief River, a long-standing meeting place and supply point for trappers before the highway arrived], where I was taken to the ladies' quarters for the night.

The next day, on to Old Fort Nelson, and I soon found out that my jobs at George's Store were many: cooking, making coffee for whoever came by, store clerk, postmaster's assistant, and, when the Georges left

---

[42] Anne Callison. "My Early Years in Fort Nelson." *Fort Nelson News*, Oct 21, 1992. Altered and expanded here and there.

to go for supplies or go on holidays, I had to manage the store and business as well. My wages went up, first from $50 per month to $75, then to $100 a month for 14 or 16 hour days, seven days a week.[43]

At first when I was working there, native trappers and others would come into the store and stay along the wall, or in the corner, staring at me. It kind of unnerved me and I commented to Mrs. George. She replied "oh they're just looking at you because you're blond!" I think I must have been the first blond woman they'd seen.

I sold a lot of souvenirs to the soldiers and construction fellows from the base, and I baked and served pie and coffee to all, fourteen to twenty pies a day! Mrs. George made many parkas and mukluks but could never keep ahead of the demand. We sold a lot of fur pieces for trimming women's coats. Spring was always very busy, as on top of the soldiers, we had trappers coming in with their winter catch of furs. I soon learned how the grading of the fur was done. Mr. George and the Hudson's Bay were the only buyers at Fort Nelson. On top of it all, if trappers did not have a place to stay, we gave them a bed and fed them.

I didn't go out much as I was scared. Mr. George, though, was a big help; he used to tell everyone I was his daughter. That gave me quite a lot of protection with all those men. I was only twenty-one and had never been in a place like Fort Nelson.

Later that year, in the summer of 1943, when business was a bit slower, Mrs. George wanted to take a trip to Whitehorse, Yukon by road, to see where this highway went! She tried to get a pass for both of us, with no success, as no women were allowed to travel the Highway. Trucks were hauling supplies to Whitehorse in convoys and Mrs. George asked some of the drivers if we could go along. One said okay but we had to take our chances. We drove with them and they timed it so that we would arrive at the BC/Yukon border at midnight.

A few miles before we came to the border, our driver stopped and said: "This is where we make the change; you girls get in the back and under the tarp." Mrs. George and I crawled into the back and squeezed right up to the front of the truck, far from the opening, then they tied the tarp down again over the load.

I could not believe this was happening; what were we doing! The

---

[43] $100 a month in 1943 is the equivalent of $1400 in 2017. Working as Anne did was no way to get rich quick, though she did have free room and board!

truck moved forward and stopped at the inspection station. A couple of officers came out with flashlights; we heard one walk around the truck as the other untied the tarp at the back and just flashed his light around the inside. Our driver, meanwhile, went in to sign some papers.

I think I froze and thawed out a couple of times in fear. Our driver came out, though, and we went onward again. We drove quite a ways before he was able to safely stop so we could get in the cab again.

We stayed at Whitehorse a couple of days to visit and explore, then on our way back we stopped at the same inspection station, where we were asked by puzzled officers how we got to Whitehorse. Mrs. George, never short for an answer, said that we flew. A good thing he did not ask to see the plane tickets! We stopped at the construction camps for meals. Everyone was really great. At Mile 710, we stayed for the night. The next morning we saw twelve bears feeding on the leftovers from the mess hall.

Scenery was beautiful all along the route. We stopped at the Liard Hot Springs, which is now a world renowned attraction.[44] It was a wonderful trip, though the road was very winding and very dusty.

Come November of 1943, some of the construction fellows working for KCB, a civilian contractor, decided they wanted to put a play together for Christmas to entertain all the workers, and they needed a couple of ladies to fill the bill. At first, I said "no," as I didn't feel comfortable going on my own; then Olive Taylor said she would go if I would. So I changed my mind and said "yes," as we would travel together to and from the construction camp. Walter Taylor and George Behn would supply the transportation, which meant dog teams as the river was not frozen deeply enough for vehicles to cross.

They named their play "Over Fourteen and Single." We had three weeks to practise our parts. Then the day before our final performance, the director said that it would make it more realistic if I would kiss the leading man at the final performance. The attendance was great; the mess hall was full for every performance.

---

[44] Liard Hotsprings is now a BC Provincial Park. It's the second largest hotsprings in Canada, and is, in effect, a warm-water muskeg in the boreal forest. The US Army Engineers first built raised walkways here in 1942, and these have been maintained and expanded, so that visitors will not harm the delicate muskeg ecosystem. Plant life there is rich for it is a microclimate that is nearly tropical. For instance, fourteen species of orchids flourish here! *(info from BC Parks)*

A couple of days later, we were approached by the Air Force officer, asking us if we would entertain the troops for New Year's. They would help us put a programme together. They would use the airplane hangar for the hall, and would build a stage at one end for us. For our programme, we had Christmas carols, recitations, mouth organ concertos, jokes—whatever we could put together for a two hour programme. We were told that 1000 people attended, some coming from as far as 100 miles away! I can still see the hangar full of people. Took the joy away from Bob Hope that year! The next spring, Fort Nelson was part of the circuit; Hollywood sent some of their entertainers up and I attended the performances as well.

Dresses were what we wore most of the time. No high heel shoes, though. We did wear slacks, when out tobogganing or horseback riding.

As well, we did have our afternoon teas. Mrs. Garbet, Mrs. Alexander, Mrs. George and any ladies that were around the town all attended. We wore our fur pieces whenever we went out.

I had my first airplane ride one day, with a U.S. Air Force pilot who landed his ski-plane on the frozen Fort Nelson River. After we were up in the air for a while, the pilot asked me how I was doing. I said that I was doing just fine. Then he asked me if I could stand a flip. So be it, the flip it was done! I learned to skate in Fort Nelson as well, on the river right outside our doors. It was the soldiers who ordered me the skates from "outside." Also, I had my first fishing experience that year, and learned to fish. The first time I caught one, I lost the fish, line and hook and all.

The Fort Nelson flood in July 1943 was a scary experience. Some families and camps had to be moved to higher ground. The river rose dramatically every spring with run-off from snow in the mountains, but some years, like 1943, were spectacular. People could tie their boats up to the hitching post outside the George's store!

One accident I remember well. It brought a lot of chuckles to the community, as it involved the only two non-military vehicles at the base, those of the RCMP and the Game Warden! Somehow, they just had to run into each other. There was little damage, and no one was injured, but it sure gave us a lot of laughs for days.

And there was a Métis fellow named Tommy Clark who had a trading post in Fort Nelson too, buying furs to sell at auction down south. When he went out, he'd leave his glass eye in the window to scare off thieves, as he couldn't use it in the winter cold. Lash Callison, always full of practical jokes, liked to tease him. He skinned a dead dog and tried to sell it to Tommy as a wolf pelt. Tommy knew fur well but he fell for it and bought that dog fur. They had a big laugh afterward.

Many people's lives have been enriched by the building of the Alaska Highway. I feel it is the greatest drawing card we have today, especially with the Liard Hot Springs, one of the largest in Canada. Many people around the world come to travel the Highway now.

To close my tale of life in Fort Nelson, I'll leave you these precious words: *As long as we have memories yesterday remains. As long as we have hope tomorrow awaits. As long as we have friendship, today is beautiful.*

Old Fort Nelson, 1942. The dark building is George's Store and Café.

US Soldiers arrive by dog team in Fort Nelson in 1942 (before Anne worked there). Outside George's Store.

Woman using the local public transit in Old Fort Nelson to cross the river!

Trapper arriving at George's Store with load of furs. Arthur George on the right.

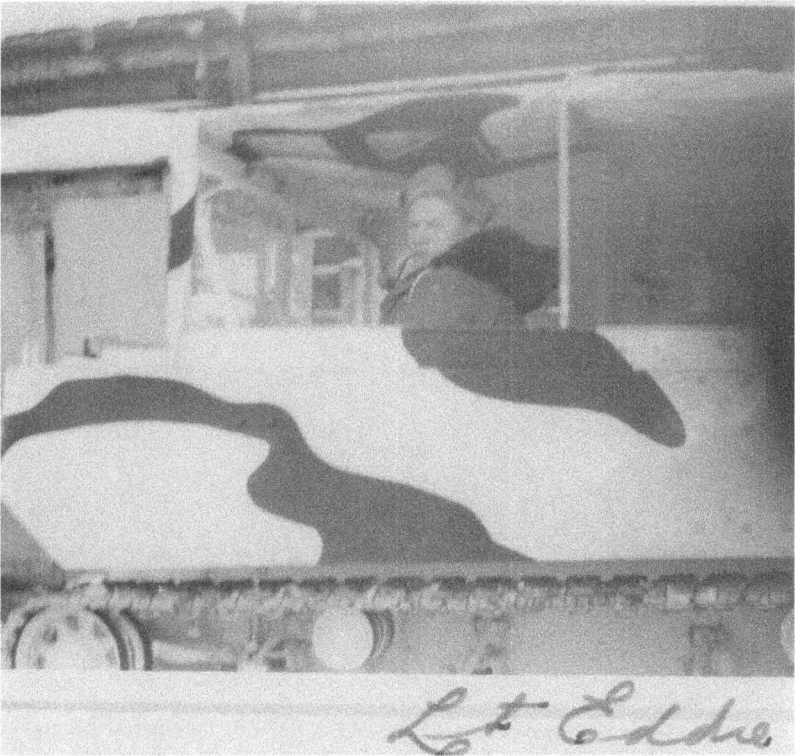

US Army Lieutenant Eddie (in Anne's writing) outside George's Store in Ft. Nelson, in the tracked "bus" used to ferry soldiers from camp to Fort Nelson.

George's Store, Fort Nelson, ~1938 (each trapper has $2-3000 worth of furs).

Arthur George arriving at Laird River (perhaps Fort Laird), earlier in the 1930s, where the Georges had a store and café for prospectors and trappers in the lands of the Acho Dene Koe, before moving to Old Fort Nelson.

Note: all the photographs in this chapter—apart from that of Lt. Eddie—come from a small black and white "Aristo" album in Anne's archives. They date from before her time in Fort Nelson, and were sold as a souvenir album at the store by the enterprising Georges.

VIGNETTE—Lodema George, Fort Nelson's First Lady

Lodema George was born in Kansas on July 12, 1890, and married Arthur George in Idaho. They went to the Peace River Country in 1920, and homesteaded near Peace Crossing. Though they didn't really like clearing land, they stayed four years, managing to make ends meet by trapping (Arthur walked ahead of the dog team and broke trail, and Lodema drove the dog sled). In 1924, fed up with sedentary life, they built a boat and headed downriver, aiming north and intent on travelling to prospect near Great Bear Lake where they had heard news of a pitchblende strike, but ended up frozen over in Fort Simpson. A trapper guided them up 200 miles up the Liard River and they trapped there at a place the native people called Drowned Snye. Their cabin was a real social centre; they put people up overnight travelling from or to Fort Liard, and Mrs. George cooked meals and her famous bread. Eventually, the industrious couple were persuaded to open a stopping place, general store, and café in Fort Liard for trappers and prospectors, where they served family-style meals for 6 at a time, 3 times a day.

In 1938, after prospecting in the Yukon and northern BC (in the winter of 1934 with Wop May at McMillan Lake south of the Nahanni in the Yukon), they moved to Old Fort Nelson, a community along the river of several hundred people, both white people involved in trapping, for the most part, and prospecting and trade, and Indigenous families, whose small village was adjacent (on lands later taken from them by the government). Old Fort Nelson, when the Georges arrived, was a remote community, accessible by water from the north or by tote-trail or dogteam from Fort St. John in the south, and all under the hand of the Catholic and protestant churches, and the Hudson's Bay Company. Mrs. George was the third white woman in the community. There they built another residence-stopping place-café, and went into business buying furs, in competition with the Hudson's Bay Company. Their services were welcomed by local trappers, Indigenous and non-Indigenous, as they were renowned for fairness and generosity. Lodema George was known as a sharp fur buyer and astute businesswoman.

Lodema was also famed for her parties and dances; people would sing, Baptiste would play guitar, and all would dance for hours on the fur grading floor! Both Indigenous and non-Indigenous folk attended. A few years later, when Old Fort Nelson's airport suddenly became home to 2000 American soldiers working to build the Alcan Highway, Mrs. George cooked and served even more meals, took on more employees (such as Anne Grendys), and still organized dances and get-togethers, teas, card games, and socials. Of the American soldiers, many, it seems, were Black soldiers from the southern States; Mrs. George noticed that they had the greatest of difficulties keeping warm, and that they didn't know green wood from dry when it came to lighting fires! "They'd come over to our place whenever they could and huddle around the stove; they were so cold, just shivering! They were awfully nice men, homesick boys." They were sick of Army fare and had wages, and would come when possible for a home-cooked meal. Carrots, lettuce, peas, turnips, cucumbers, green tomatoes, cabbage, cauliflower and potatoes grew in Mrs. George's gardens by the river, and her meals were fresh and flavourful, accompanied by homemade pickles. Dry goods and other supplies were shipped in by wagon over the trail before the highway went in and sometimes were lost falling through ice into rivers. To fly in supplies cost 25c a pound.

By this time, Mrs. George's table held twelve people at once. She cooked for soldiers, trappers, and travellers, roasted innumerable turkeys for Christmas and New Year's, baked her famous bread, served up pie and coffee, acted as the postmistress, sewed fur coats and fur collars, mukluks and purses, for sale to soldiers and contractors up working on the Alcan Highway, and met and knew thousands of people. You couldn't have found a society matron more known or appreciated in New York City or Paris!

Rumour says that on special occasions the local bootlegger would borrow the priest's car and arrive at George's with supplies for the party. On a more sober note, Lodema George was also instrumental in building Fort Nelson's first school.

In 1945, with the Alcan highway a few miles from the old Fort and on the airport side of the river, isolating the older community, a new town sprang up at the highway to serve those going through. The Georges built a second grocery store and restaurant in the new Fort Nelson as well, which they ran until they sold it in 1954. Arthur George had unfortunately suffered a stroke that year, and Mrs. George wasn't able to run both places. The store in new Fort Nelson became the Foodmart (Fort Nelson Realty now).

When Arthur died in January 1957, it was a huge blow for Mrs. George. She continued to run the store at the Old Fort until May 2, 1958, when she lost her store, home, and all her belongings in a terrible fire. There was, apparently, no means of fighting the conflagration; everyone went to see what they could do, and could only watch the venerable store burn, in shock and horror. It was the end of an era in Old Fort Nelson. "All I had left was the clothes on my back," Mrs. George said. "I was lost, I didn't know what to do. I did a little bit of everything after that: cooked at the hospital, helped out at the other stores."

Lodema George continued to travel, and in 1965, at the urging of friends, and feeling that the arrival of the oil industry had irrevocably changed the Fort Nelson she knew, she moved to a seniors' apartment in Bridgeland in Calgary. Anne continued to travel to visit her, and Anne's sister Mary and family, who lived in Calgary, looked out for her as a precious member of their own family. Lodema George formed new friendships, and kept busy. Mary's children remember her at holiday dinners, full of enthralling stories. She returned to Fort St. John in 1980, to be close to her family nearby, and continued to visit Fort Nelson. She died on March 18 1987 in Fort St. John at the age of 96. There'll never be another woman like her, and clearly her independent and self-sufficient ways rubbed off on Anne Callison, who remained a lifelong friend.[45]

---

[45] Info from *The Fort Nelson Story*, and *Fort Nelson News*: "Lodema George leaves Fort Nelson" Jan 27, 1965; "Pioneer Profile-Lodema George" Feb 4, 1981; "Obituary-Lodema George" April 15, 1987 (FN Archives), and from my memory.

Love and Marriage
March 1943 to July 10, 1944

With the Alcan Highway built, and the P.R.A. in charge in 1943 of widening, straightening, and surfacing the pioneer road using civilian contractors, military convoys began using the highway to supply airports along the way to Alaska, in defense of the North American continent. It was still not safe for any vehicle to travel solo, as there were no services or gas stations: no help if a person had a breakdown. Gasoline was only available to authorized users, pumped from big drums at the construction and maintenance camps along the way. Truck convoys also carried barrels of gasoline, along with mechanics, tools, and parts. Permission from US Military authorities was required to be on the highway, which was only opened to civilian traffic in 1948.

Anne worked long days at George's Store, so she socialized by and large as she worked, making sure everyone was served. The outside world was very male-oriented and military. Anne was scared to be out alone (and no wonder). If she did accept a date to go to a dance or other event, Mrs. George or the Highways Administrator would go along with her.

Given that the soldiers in 1943 had more time for recreation than did those in 1942, there were often entertainments, shows, movies, and dances held at the air base, and the presence of the community's young women was welcomed. There were lots of invitations! Every woman in the area was invited to attend.

When John Callison came off the trapline to Fort Nelson in the spring of 1943, he met Anne Grendys at George's Store. It was the meeting of two people whose *paths* had already crossed (though John was not present) back in 1929! As the months went on, the pair did start to see more of each other. John was always gentlemanly and respectful, and though he had so many different experiences, he was not a boastful man, nor did he need to be the centre of attention. He was not a controlling person, but a listening one. He had respect and love for the natural world, for horses in particular, and shared his knowledge to help others. He was the kind of man who pitched in. All of this couldn't help but impress Anne. Anne claims they weren't courting at that point, though, and says simply that "we were seeing each other." Anne did go to a few of the events at the airport at John's invitation, with the Hudson's Bay Company assistant manager along as chaperone. They'd only really known each other a few months, and Anne had boyfriends down around Saskatoon Mountain where her family lived; she wasn't yet thinking of settling down, at least not at Fort Nelson. It was John doing the pursuing, she says.

VIGNETTE—He Was So Handsome!

Anne tells the story on video of her first meeting with John, one day when he walked into George's Trading Post in Fort Nelson in 1943: "He stood in the door, quiet, with his load of furs, just waiting by the wall, as the Indians did. He was really dark from the sun and working outside. I went to Mrs. George who was in the back, and told her: 'there's an Indian here just came in with his furs.' Mrs. George got up and looked out and went and served the man, and when she came back, she told me, 'That man's not Indian; that's John, one of the Callison boys.'"

In the video, the voice of the interviewer proposes: "I guess it wasn't quite love at first sight." Anne, in the limelight, answers modestly, "I don't know, maybe."

But when she related the story of first meeting John to her nephew, Bill Moure, in the 1970s, she added: "The minute he walked in the door I knew: I am going to marry that man."

"He was so handsome."

As spring wore on in 1944, Anne began looking forward to going back to Huallen and up to the Grendys homestead to see her parents and to Grande Prairie to see her sister. Mary had been ill and was recovering from surgery, an arduous process as there was no penicillin for civilians during the war (antibiotics did not yet exist). Their brother Joe, who worked on the farm with their dad, was in the Army. His absences in Petawawa, Ontario, to receive munitions training, and in other postings in southern Alberta and in Saskatchewan, meant their parents had to run the farm on their own. Meanwhile, the Georges were hankering after a vacation, so Lodema and Anne struck a bargain. Anne would have July 1944 off to go home, and she promised to return to manage the store and café in the month of August, so the Georges could get away. They'd come to rely on Anne and her skills with all parts of their business, not just cooking. She was a pragmatic and energetic employee, always organized and organizing those around her.

So in July, Anne headed back down to her family north of Huallen. John, who had a car, volunteered to drive her down to the farm himself, and Anne had agreed to that idea. Then she found out about another group headed south, and went with them instead!

She did stop overnight in Dawson Creek, not at the hospital this time but at John's mother's house, as arranged by John. In order to make ends meet, and provide a needed service, Dora Callison rented rooms in her house to young women who needed accommodation. So Anne met John's mom, who in turn had a chance to learn more about this young woman on whom her son had his eye. Then Anne headed onward to the Grendys farm.

Well, John was not taking her departure lightly! He came down from Fort Nelson to the farm in that car of his to visit Anne almost right away. It may have been that he realized the risk that, once home, this young woman Anne might never come back up to Fort Nelson. He was aware too that she had already had serious boyfriends in her home area near Huallen, and didn't want to give them a chance, or Anne a chance to forget him!

In any case, John showed up almost immediately in Alberta. So, says Anne, that was when they *really* started "seeing each other." They courted for about two weeks, and John lured her off on a trip south to go see the Calgary Stampede, with John's sister Mollie Callison and Clarence Cottam—Mollie's future husband—as chaperones. After this whirlwind courtship, John and Anne married on July 10, 1944 in the Catholic Church, before they got to the Stampede. Anne playfully says: "We looked at the cost of hotel rooms on arrival in Edmonton and decided it would be cheaper to pay for one room rather than two. We made our decision, and got married."

Good to her word, Anne returned in August 1944 to work at the store in Old Fort Nelson while the Georges took their vacation.

In the month she was working in Fort Nelson, John went to the Kledo River where he built more cabins along his trapline, and their first family home, using milled lumber salvaged from the structures left the previous year by the 35th Engineers. Now Anne could go along with him in the winter, and have more comfort and privacy. When the Georges returned in September to the store, Anne Callison left their employment to begin married life with her beloved John.

In September 1944, they headed together to Dawson Creek to purchase and prepare all the supplies for a winter on the trapline, staying at John's mother's house. They soon headed north on the highway to the boreal forest and floodplain where the Kledo meets the Muskwa River, to live for the winter in Weasel City and run the trapline together.

"So I went out on the trapline with John," Anne remembers. She pauses for a moment, then looks up and says: "Oh my dear!"

July 10, 1944. Miss Anne Grendys becomes Mrs. John Callison—a day to celebrate! Clarence Cottam, John, Mollie Callison, with Anne in the foreground.

Winter on the Trapline:
Pelts Smell Bad! Pelts Smell Good!

We're talking here of an era before ATVs, jet boats, snowmobiles, cell or satellite phones, electricity, refrigeration: machines and technologies now common on the rivers and ice and soils of the Peace River district. *Think silence.* Think the cracking of spruce branches in the winter as the sun warms the surface of the bark, the chorus of boreal chickadees, redpolls, downy woodpeckers, and whiskey jacks, the night hoot of the great grey owl. Moose were even more common then; their favoured terrain then as now was the wetlands of valleys, the muskeg of sphagnum mosses, standing waters, little rivulets and creeks, standing aspen and birch, and where it is wettest, willow bushes. Berries, so many berries, all with their seasons and all rich in nutrients. An ecosystem of light and air and soil sustains us as we trek from the northernmost reaches of the great interior plains that link northeast BC to Alberta, and head out from the old town of Fort Nelson at the confluence of the Muskwa and Fort Nelson Rivers—known as *Tthek'eneh Kúe*, the place of the Tse'Kene, people of the rocks— to rise westward into the great boreal forest, toward the great mountains. Here all rivers join in their valleys to flow north into the Arctic Ocean. We are in the ancient lands of the Tse'Kene, Dane-zaa, and Dogrib peoples.

In early November of 2017 as this text was written, the first snowfall came and left 55 cm in Fort St. John, to the south. The winter ice has not yet come, though, to crack and release icepans into the rivers before the pans freeze together and the ice deepens.

Outside at night, the aurora borealis shimmers its huge electric curtains of light: the Northern Lights, brilliant messengers to our tiny planet sent to all earth's beings from the sun itself. The first computer screen, perhaps: mesmerizing. In the forests, even the grizzly bears look up to their light. The Dall sheep climb rocky precipices in the shadows they throw. The wind sounds its low and sweet moan through the ragged spruce, which creak in the dark as they bend.

Dogs were first introduced to this area in 1893. They were working animals, adept at carrying supplies, and soon every family owned several. A dog, it is said, can carry twenty-five to thirty kilograms and travel twenty-five kilometres a day, and a team of four dogs or so can move a moosehide and wood sleigh quickly across frozen muskeg, with the driver riding the runners at the back or out in the front on snowshoes, breaking trail. Winters made travel easier, even if the temperatures could plunge to 60 below.

It was only with the arrival of settler-farmers to the northern plains and forests, in about 1920, that horses began to be seen more frequently. They were not very apt for muskeg; trails had to be cut to enable them to pass through wet and tangled territory, though they made good time in open valleys. For horse-drawn wagons to pass, even wider trails had to be cut and at least partly packed with road materials found nearby, so these trails were rare until the 1950s, when the area started to be crisscrossed by seismic lines exploring for oil and gas, for "the grease of the big animals underground," as Dane-zaa history has it. As well, food for horses had to be hauled with them, as once into boreal forest and wetlands, there were few grasses. So it was, at first, that the rivers, clear of brush and fast-moving, were the major transport corridors for the newcomers: bark and hide canoes, as well as flat-bottomed scows, rafts, barges, and other light craft built on the riverbanks out of whipsawn lumber were all paddled and poled long before fuel existed in sufficient quantity for the settlers to use motors. Indigenous people built rafts as well, though the inland trails were their preferred routes.

Animal trapping had been a way of life since pre-European contact times. It was a source of pelts and also of food when large game was scarce. With the arrival of the Cree, who worked for and preceded the first European traders, came lifestyle changes: guns, stoves, flour, baking powder, sugar, bolts of cloth to sew clothing. There were few white men and fewer white women in this north. Mostly the white trappers went out to trap and live alone on their lines or in their home cabins, though in some cases, wives did work alongside them. Indigenous family groups always worked together; they hunted and trapped in the winter for food and trade, following seasonal rounds to avoid depleting game. In 1925, the BC government began to require registration of traplines by both white and Indigenous trappers. As Hugh Brody and Brenda Ireland testify, this was contrary to the treaty that gave its signatories free run of their territories forever for traditional activities. The province seemed to feel, in the fashion of white lawmaking, that regulation helped avoid conflict, but it also allowed prime trapping territory to be claimed by newcomers, who had no hesitation about the new laws and who understood the land to be open to them within the limits set by law. The Federal government, which alone dealt with Indigenous relations, never acted to protect treaty rights, despite First Nations complaints and pleas. Meanwhile, at the confluence of the Muskwa and the Kledo where the Callisons trapped, Indigenous and white trappers co-existed respectfully. On the ground, they worked hard and safely to care for the land and animals. Newcomers were still so few that no one could then imagine the disruptions that later influxes of people would bring.

No one was bored. No one recalls being lonely. Why do we always ask pioneers if they were bored or lonely? Our lives of comfort leave us time to be bored; I guess! With all our modern distractions, our phones and toys, we fail to imagine the satisfactions people felt when immersed in the rhythms of the seasons and the work each entailed. For northern people, there was much to do to keep going all winter: the house had to be cleaned; wood chopped for fuel for warmth and cooking; animals had to be skinned and their fur stretched and scraped and dried; berries and medicinal plants had to be gathered; kitchen gardens planted, tended, harvested, and the vegetables and fruit preserved by canning in jars or by being dug into the ground in small caverns known as root cellars: the earliest refrigerators. Bear fat was rendered into lard for cooking fat; it is said to make the best pie crust ever! Water had to be hauled and heated; dogs cared for and fed. Meat was hunted, hung, cut, dried or canned, and stored. Bread was baked. Clothes mended and sewn. Mukluks sewn, and jackets. Toques, scarves, blankets and sweaters were knitted. If small children were present, there was even more work, more laundry, more to cook, and more urgent need to keep houses warm.

John Callison had learned to trap animals for fur in his teenage years, working with his father and brothers further south, as a way of making money in an era when the toils of clearing land and farming brought scant returns and no cash. He didn't mind long winters, and the isolation to him was a chance to be in nature and to work at a natural rhythm that he'd long learned, aided by dogs and horses, and supported by whoever else was in the bush. He knew how to map and survey, how to read animal movements and winds, how to read their tracks and scat and know what they were eating, and if they were hungry or sated. He was able to find his way, to keep warm, and to work carefully so as to avoid accidents. Like all who shared this working life, he helped others; he'd go days out of his way to deliver an urgent message or get health assistance for someone fallen ill.

In 1933, when he was 24 years old, well before the Alaska Highway was built or even imagined, John leased his own registered trapline along the Kledo River and nearby watersheds, about 50 km northwest of Fort Nelson. His brother Lash, and cousin George Lynch, also trapped in the area, and had surveyed their own lines. Brother Dennis joined them a couple of years later for a winter. They built home cabins close to each other, where the Kledo met the Muskwa, and called the little group of houses Weasel City. They traded their furs in Fort Nelson at the Hudson Bay Company in the 1930s, and later, at Arthur and Lodema George's Store, which opened in 1938 and offered better prices than the Hudson's Bay and more services to trappers. Trapping provided important income for John's homestead and his family, particularly in the 1930s when there was no other work and no market for farm products. People farmed in the Depression so as to live, and trapped to earn money to afford the cost of farming!

John with dog team, 1942.

John worked his trapline for many years after he married Anne and they had started a family. Anne comments on the high price for furs at the time: "Trapping was where the money was. You could make more in a month trapping than most people did in a year. In the Depression, a lot of people would work and only have $150-$200 a month to show for it, but John would go out there and after a couple of weeks come back with $2-3000 worth of fur."[46]

After Anne and John were married in 1944 and Anne had fulfilled her responsibilities to the Georges in Fort Nelson, she accompanied John first to Dawson Creek to prepare supplies, then up to the Kledo and the trapline. On reaching John's home cabin, though, it wasn't all joy. The newlyweds each had some moments of utter dismay!

For her part, Anne reacted strongly to the smell of pelts that imbued the cabin, and told her new husband that she thought the pelts really smelled bad. He was startled at this, and he replied to her, in his patient way, that to him it was a good smell. So Anne tried at first to tolerate the smell; the Indigenous trappers too told her that it was a good smell. She couldn't bear living with it; it made her practically gag. She had to do something, so she set to cleaning the house thoroughly. Well, the house still smelled bad, she says. So she cleaned the whole house again, and aired it out even more to "catch the smell."

"And then finally it was good," she said. What a relief! Lucky for all of us readers (for this book would be very different if it were otherwise!), with help from her new intensive housekeeping standards, Anne finally could stand the smell of her first married home.

She still tells the story of her first morning in the home cabin as a wife. It was the start of a whole new life for her, and she was excited to be there, and wanting to do things to please her husband. She asked John what he wanted for breakfast, and he said he'd like some bannock. She hadn't ever made bannock before, or cooked on such a stove as the small one in the cabin, but she followed John's instructions. As a newlywed wife, she was expected to do the cooking, and she did love to cook. So she cooked her first bannock. "At breakfast," she said, "John ate quietly, and I was hoping he liked the meal. I was nervous about my bannock and from the way he was eating it, I could tell it wasn't quite right. John finished off his plate without complaining, then got up and, without a word, scraped the leftover bannock from the pan and threw it out the door for the dogs. But even the dogs wouldn't eat it! Oh my," she said, "I was mortified! John's bannock was a lot better than mine, but I soon learned."

They laughed about that one many a time. Bannock, after all, was one of those dishes that everyone who lived on the trapline learned to

---

[46] Melanie Robinson, op. cit.

make. It was good and nourishing pan bread, could be made on top of a wood stove or over a fire, and didn't require an oven. Probably John Callison's father Fred had learned how to cook bannock from Alex Gladue, when he was first learning how to trap and manage a trapline near the Pouce Coupe prairie, and John learned from his father, before teaching Anne.

Once out on the trapline, Anne was confronted with many situations where she had to learn new skills, and learn she did. She'd never tried on snowshoes before, but when John advised her there was no way she could walk around in such deep snow in boots alone, she let him strap the long shoes of moosehide and wood to her feet, and learned to walk miles in them. Anne remembers being frightened at first when John asked her to drive the dog team; she objected that she didn't know how, and was afraid of having an accident, of hurting herself or John, or—disaster!—the dogs. John calmly told her to step up on the back runners and hold on, looking ahead at the dogs! He showed her how to use the brake, and how to call commands, and reassured her. As long as the dogs were okay, he said, she'd be fine; the dogs know what they're doing. They knew where the trapline was, and where to go and when to stop. Anne said, "I'd got all worried, but just had to decide then not to worry, just do it, and so I learned."

They had an area of about 800 square kilometres (300^2 miles) to cover, and checking the trapline would take about a week. The first trip each year took longer, as the traps had to be set up. "The first time I went out with John," said Anne, "my legs were so sore from walking! But after the second time, I could run a race against anyone."

Anne soon learned to use a hunting rifle. She shot a bear and skinned it on her own, and later another bear. When asked about the bears and the reason for their fate, she said they were too close to the house, and of one she said simply: "He was working against me." Anne expected even the bears to bend to her will!

She also shot wolves, otter, and beaver. She learned to use long snowshoes deep in the woods and on the rivers, how to cross ice safely, and how to best break trail, and she'd drive the dog team out on the line while John walked in front to break trail in the heavy snow.

Anne also shot and killed moose on two occasions. One time, the game warden came along to the cabin right after she'd killed one. "Oh, Anne," he said to her, on seeing the moose hanging. "You haven't got a license!" She replied, "Oh, well, I would have got one, but I didn't know

I was going to kill a moose!" He let her off the hook. She remembers the game warden now simply as a "good Catholic."

In the spring, the Callisons would take up the traps, store them and the cabin away, and leave the trapline for Fort Nelson with their catch of furs, and with their horses and dogs if they weren't being cared for by a neighbour summering there. From that point, they would head south toward Fort St. John, to the homestead at Murdale. There, John would plant crops, clear land, grow hay to feed his horses, and they would gradually make improvements together.

During their initial winter together on the trapline, in 1944-45, Anne Callison became pregnant with their first child. "Once I got in the family way," said Anne, "I stayed home after that." In later winters, she stayed in the home cabin, which was close to the highway. Spring and summer were spent "south" on the homestead beside Montney Creek.

Pat, Dennis, John, Lash, Lynch, July 1945, Dawson Creek, at their mother's funeral.

That first spring coming out from the trapline, in 1945, the couple went directly down to Dawson Creek, the town at the end of the rail line that had boomed as a result of the building of the Alcan, going from 500 residents before the war to a postwar population of 4000. John's mother Dora was by now very ill, and Anne went to live with her and take care of her, while John travelled back and forth between Dawson Creek and the farm at Murdale. The elder Mrs. Callison was fighting cancer, and despite an operation and Anne's nursing comforts, Dora Callison passed away on July 25, 1945.[47] In the last month, Anne had help with her nursing Dora at home, as on July 21 she had given birth to their firstborn son, Adley John Callison. Meeting wee Adley, the next generation, was one of Dora's final joys before she passed away.

After Adley came along, Anne stayed at the home cabin on the Kledo River instead of accompanying John on the dogsled to check and set traps. The house was near where there were beaver. Anne never got lonely, she says, when John was gone trapping, because she was too busy! On top of all the labour of keeping the house warm, water carried and heated, kindling chopped, food cooked, and clothes sewn, there was the new baby. Oh the water Anne had to boil to wash diapers! Anyone with a growing infant knows you don't get much time to think of loneliness.

Anne remembers John paying the doctor with beaver and muskrat furs instead of cash. Her children, as they grew, drank canned evaporated milk instead of fresh, something that always astonished the city cousins. I remember my aunt Anne stocking up on flats of canned milk when she visited her sister in Calgary. I myself couldn't abide the taste of it, but I knew my cousins liked it, and for me it was a sign of country life.

The Indigenous people were good people, Anne recalls, and they always had good relations with them—principally the Dane-ẕaa who lived close to them at Montney until after the war, and others who worked traplines near them further north. Anne, asked for memories, remembers one woman who was put under pressure to convert to Catholicism from her traditional religion, and she didn't want to change and stood by her decision. Said Anne, admiringly, "she had her own ways and was true to them."

---

[47] Dora Elton Callison née Lynch: born March 1879, Greenbrier County, West Virginia–died 25 July 1945, Dawson Creek, BC.

Anne Callison at Weasel City or Fort Nelson, 1944. Always stylish!

Anne holding Adley, late 1945, and pregnant with Wayne.

The house of Anne and John Callison, whether on the trapline or at the farm, was always open to others. Distances between communities were long, and hotels just did not exist outside of trading post communities. "We took in a lot of people," Anne said. She got to know everyone, wherever she was.

Her eldest son Adley remembers staying with his maternal grandparents, Nelly and Tom Grendys, in Fort Nelson, when it came time for him to start Grade One in 1951, while his parents were out on the trapline. Nelly and Tom, retired from the farm, had relocated to go look after Adley. Tom even worked as a mess man at the Canadian Army base, and his ID card says he was 62. In fact, he was 72! It wasn't the first time Tom had shed years from his age to avoid being passed over as too old.

In the years following Wayne Frederick Callison's birth on August 22, 1946 in Fort St. John, near the Murdale homestead, it became clear that the Callisons would need to live where their children could go to Catholic school (John had converted to Catholicism on marrying Anne, and Anne was firm in her faith), and that a winter life on the trapline as a family was not sustainable. With Wayne's entry into school about to occur as well, the family moved to Dawson Creek, where in August 1952, Notre Dame School had opened its new building—repurposed from US Army buildings left after the highway was built.

What did Anne like best about life in the bush? "Oh, everything," she says. "The work was hard, but I sure enjoyed it." John had money coming in, and Anne kept other aspects of their family life organized. The couple never had any big disagreements, says Anne. "I liked the trapline better than the farm," she recalls. "But what I miss most about life in the bush is the wild bird orchestra. Since I am an early riser, mornings were the best. It seems every bird in the woods would take its turn singing. Woodpeckers were the drummers."

Weasel City, 1930s, cabin and cache. John's buildings in the 1940s were more modern, as he also had used salvaged lumber, from the US 35th Engineers highway camp built at the Kledo River during Alaska Highway construction in 1942.

John with a beaver, and inflatable boat, early 1940s, at the Kledo River.

Adley Callison, winter 1945-46 on a dogsled at the Kledo River.

First winter's catch of furs, 1945 February or March, at their house by the Kledo.

Anne and John with 1945 catch of furs, about to head to Fort Nelson. John is holding a string of marten pelts. At the left in the background is the Alaska highway bridge across the Kledo River (now called Kledo Creek).

Anne displays marten (sometimes called sable) furs from a winter of trapping with John on the Kledo, outside their home, clean laundry hanging in the background!

Callison Motel, Dawson Creek:
Raising a Family

Callison Motel, Dawson Creek, after construction was completed in 1951.

In 1952, when the older boys, Adley and Wayne, were both old enough to be in school, Anne and John moved south to Dawson Creek. The city had a population of 3500 people then, and welcomed tourists and truckers to the Alaska Highway, of which it was now known as Mile 0. 1952 saw the first asphalt paving of downtown streets, though concrete sidewalks came later, and dirt streets remained common for many more years. The timber industry was the primary industry of resource extraction in the area, and it was the railhead of the Northern Alberta Railways, so a prime shipping point for goods and grain.

The Callisons looked around for a way to make a living together and provide stability for their young family in the city, while still letting John work on his winter trapline, and farm the homestead at Murdale.

In this post-war period, one of the dominant economic changes affecting ordinary people was the advent of the affordable family automobile. Tens of thousands of people were buying their first family car, and many of those were taking advantage of the car to explore new places. They could pack their supplies and food, and keep their children in a confined area, and take off on the road, stopping wherever they wished! All over Canada and the United States, to meet these new family travellers, enterprising people were building motels. "Motel" is a contraction of "motor hotel," a hotel you arrive at by car. The 1950s were the heyday of motels; they lined every highway on the way into towns and cities. Their one- or two-storey profiles and parking lots became iconic in the landscape. Years later, when freeways and expressways started to bypass towns, and chain box hotels took over, the use of motels would decline. But in the 1950s and 60s, they were in their prime, and anyone driving into a town at night passed an impressive row of them, marked by neon signs lit up with VACANCY or NO VACANCY. There was no internet, and no need in most cases to reserve a motel room in advance by looking it up in a printed guidebook and phoning. Long-distance calls were expensive! You just pulled up when you were tired and rented a room when you saw a VACANCY sign on your way into town.

The Callisons built and opened a motel in Dawson Creek, right at the beginning of the heyday, thinking to take advantage of the increased number of visitors and truckers up the Alaska Highway, curious about this war road into the unknown, and also meet the accommodation needs of those working in the mining and timber industries, and in the gas and oil fields that boomed later.

The Callison Motel was the first motel accommodation in Dawson Creek that included private indoor bathrooms in every room. It had eight rental units in four buildings, plus a building with another four units. As well there was the house in which the Callisons lived (visible at the left in the photo on page 109), which also held the motel office, and laundry facilities. In the early years, there were gas pumps out front as well. Sometime later, between 1962 and 1964, the operation was renamed the Central Motel. The Callisons ran the business until 1972. It still exists in 2017, now with RV hookups, kitchenettes, and an attached RV Park.

Running a motel came naturally to Anne and John, who were raised in a culture of hospitality. As well, there were lots of successful examples around them, as many other members of their families were also early hoteliers, building and running motels. We've mentioned that Anne's older brother Alex Grendys ran the Spring Water Motel in Ithaca, NY for .years. And in the next chapter, we'll look at the lodges along the Alaska Highway, one of which was run by John's brother Dennis, who had his hotelier start in Rolla, BC running the Columbia Hotel with his wife, and another of which, the Rancheria, was built and run by John's sister Doris and her husband William "Bud" Simpson, a status Tahltan (Nahanni) from Telegraph Creek, one of whose grandfathers had been a Hudson's Bay trader. Doris and Bud met during the Callison trek of 1935 to Dease Lake, the trip immortalized in Daisy Callison's book. Mollie and Pat and their spouses also ran lodges.

Anne and John's youngest son Darcey Bright was born in Dawson Creek in 1953, and the Callison Motel was his childhood landscape. Their home was always full of neighbours dropping by for coffee and to sample Anne's baking—I recall her as the champion of coffee cakes and butter tarts—and there was always the bustle of young women working in the motel as chambermaids, and the bell ringing in the front office announcing the arrival of tourists. Their living room was a place of peace and quiet for parents and children, and there was a play area for children in the basement complete with dart games and others. The three Callison children all thrived.

Peace Glen Hotel in Hudson Hope, early 1960s.

In the early 1960s, John was also a partner in the consortium that built the modern Peace Glen Hotel in Hudson's Hope, a coal mining town and transport hub west of Fort St. John. The sternwheeler D.A.

Thomas docked here, and it was on an Indigenous canoe route into Alberta and up to the Northwest Territories. The town was experiencing a boom during the construction of the Portage Mountain Dam on the Peace River. The dam facilities opened in 1967 as the W.A.C. Bennett Dam, and began producing electrical power the following year, one of the first examples of the North Peace providing power to the south of the province and, later, to the oil extraction industry in Northern Alberta. The population of Hudson's Hope, however, never really grew after the completion of the dam, and the Peace Glen was not as successful as John had hoped, and he soon bailed out of the venture. The hotel remained a popular local spot, however, until it was lost in a fire in 1984, rebuilt, then taken by fire one last time in 2008.

Even after building the Callison Motel, John continued to trap every spring on his Kledo River trapline. His son Wayne worked with him a few years, trapping beaver in late April and May when the pelts are at their prime, until leaving for UBC in 1963. John farmed up at Murdale on the family homestead as well.

In 1962 and 1963, Anne's attention turned back south to her Alberta home, and she drove back and forth to Grande Prairie frequently to look after her mother Nelly, who was ill with the liver cancer that would take her life. Nelly died on November 22, 1963, the same tragic day in which the radio news announced the assassination of US President John F. Kennedy. It seemed, looking south from the Peace River, that the closer a person got to so-called "civilization" and its sources, the less "civil" the world was.

John, Anne and their son Wayne; John and Anne at the Central Motel, 1967.

In 1972, with their children grown and even Darcey now at university down south in BC, Anne and John sold the motel in Dawson Creek and, after a few years, moved up to Fort St. John to be nearer the farm at Murdale. In 1973, John purchased more land in the Montney area to expand the original homestead, and over time developed what was known admiringly as "a fair-sized spread," three sections in total. He was back where he was happiest, working the land in the countryside he loved.

Around that time, John's nephew Bill, a young teenager, came up from Calgary in the summers to work with John, and learn the ways of farming, fishing, and hunting. John told Bill at that time that if he could do it all over again, he'd never have gone into the motel business at all. "He would have just gone into raising cattle at Murdale with his boys," Bill says, remembering. Aside from the trapline and horses, the homestead was what he loved.

In 1975, construction of a second dam on the mighty Peace River began downstream from the Bennett Dam. The Peace Canyon Dam was opened in September 1980. In between those two dates, in 1977, Anne's beloved father Tom Grendys died, a short time after celebrating his 100th birthday at the Hythe Pioneer Home with a special cake, surrounded by family.

The era when the Peace River Country was characterized by its immigrants was coming to an end. Their memories of the Old Country, their sadness at the ferocities of war in the East of Europe that destroyed their native communities and neighbours, were slowly lost. Even the families of their children were now grown; many had left for other opportunities, and as the old grandparents died, mementoes and letters in strange languages and alphabets were discarded. Many stories vanished into silence. And only some of their descendants stayed to form part of the next generation that would shape the history of the Peace.

Central Motel in Dawson Creek, 2015.

Callison and Moure cousins at the Central Motel: Adley, Ken Moure, Darcey, Erín, Wayne, with Bill in front, 1961.

Guides, Prospectors, Farmers, Trappers, Cooks
The Era of the Lodges on the Alaska Highway

With the Alaska Highway having opened up the North Peace and made it easier for newcomers to enter territory to hunt, there was increased curiosity and demand from sports hunters, particularly from the USA. Their goal was not to feed their families, but to take trophies. The territories where they came to hunt were those that Treaty 8 had guaranteed to the Dane-ẕaa, Tsek'ene, and other Indigenous peoples for them to hunt, fish, and camp as they always had, activities key to their livelihood and to the health of the land for future generations. The arrival of hunters was thus viewed with dismay by the first peoples, as was the increased presence of roads to remove timber or do seismic testing, for such roads meant even more interference with animal habitat. Gradually, the BC government, tasked with overseeing hunting and fishing, began to respond to concerns about game harvesting with regulations and licenses. These were not always entirely successful, and often led to Treaty disputes that laid bare, once again, the two different understandings of treaty rights and responsibilities.

With the war over, and with all the highway publicity attracting American hunters, Lash and Dennis Callison started their own business guiding those visitors who primarily sought moose in the lowlands, stone sheep in the mountains, caribou, and bear. They were away for weeks, at times. On occasion, John worked for them, as did Indigenous guides and wranglers, particularly since the Callisons were concerned about trophy hunters leaving the meat of the animals to go to waste. With Indigenous hunters present, use of the meat for food was assured. Leaving meat behind, and disrespectful treatment of the bush and its resources, was something that John viewed badly. If guides there had to be, John figured, he'd better contribute, as better him than someone who would cause animal suffering or more damage to the land. So he too worked at times on the hunts that took place after harvest and before the late October snows that marked the start of trapping season.

At one point, John wanted Anne to go along on some of the hunts, and though hesitant at first, she went. She managed the camp, looking after the horses, and cooking. When asked if she worried about being out in the bush alone while everyone else was hunting, she replied: "I just worried about my cooking!" She did this for a couple of autumn hunting seasons.

The experience she gained in cooking for groups—planning, improvising, timing, budgeting—did Anne in good stead later, as she organized many community dinners through the CWL (Catholic Women's League) and other civic groups in both Dawson Creek and Fort St. John over the years, serving up to 200 people at a time at banquets held for many different occasions. Anne had a practical sense that couldn't be beat, and could size up a banquet job quickly, jotting menus in her notebook and making shopping lists for everything from turkeys to hams to dinner rolls, creating precise schedules for all the steps in preparation, serving, and clean up, for the number of volunteers needed, and who needed to be called to give the speeches and offer entertainment! Some of her banquet records are among the papers Anne kept in her archive, showing how much she valued this part of her life.

Lash, Dennis, and John Callison, who had all worked on the Alaska Highway, foresaw then that their lives as trappers would never be the same. Amid all the changes, they watched for opportunities. Lash staked out ten acres at Mile 422, and bought the buildings from Camp 138, home to the Jupp Construction crews from York, Ontario who had worked refining the highway (BC construction outfits were at the time too small to take on highway contracts). Dennis and Lash Callison knew the area well; they had used the Toad River site as a stopping place when guiding highway surveyors in 1942, after having travelled the area in 1935 with their father on a summer trip across the Cassiar Range.

By war's end, Lash and Winnie Callison were living at Mile 301 with their two sons, Garry and Grant.[48] Dennis and Marj Callison (née Clay; her mother was Rosalie Clay, wife of William Clay, Rolla area pioneer[49];

---

[48] Lynch Callison and his wife had four small children at Rose Prairie; all four toddlers tragically lost their lives in a house fire on December 10, 1942 when their father was off trapping: Dennis, Marlene, Corrine, and Mary Lynn. In a later family tragedy, Lash and Winnie's son Grant drowned in a car mishap on June 11, 1961.

[49] The youngest son of Rosalie Clay, Marj Callison's brother Allan, a rodeo rider who worked for Imperial Oil, was left paraplegic in 1959 after a vehicle accident near Drumheller, AB. When he was sent for rehabilitation to the Calgary rehab centre in the former TB Sanatorium in Bowness, Anne Callison asked her sister Mary, who lived in Calgary, to visit him regularly and bring him news. I remember visiting Allan; he was the first person I'd seen in a wheelchair. Allan was considered family; I knew him as a handsome distant cousin, just 26 years old at the time. Such are the ties of the Peace River!

Marj met Dennis while boarding at Dora Callison's in Dawson Creek) married in 1944 and operated the Columbia Hotel in the then-bustling small town of Rolla BC, before moving north to Toad River.

Thus it was that in 1947, while John and Anne were trapping in the winter and living at Murdale in the summer, Lash and Dennis and their wives opened the Toad River Lodge for travellers and hunters at Mile 422, complete with café and gas pumps. The lodge generated its own electricity (and did so until 2012), had outhouses for delicate matters, and offered basic sleeping arrangements. It also served as a stopping place, gas station, café, and garage for repairs and tire changes. At times rooms were shared, particularly when bad weather took vehicles off the road. The Callison quartet kept horses, and guided hunters as well. Lash worked with them for the first few years. In the first issue in 1949 of *The Milepost*, the classic manual of resources and conditions along the Alaska Highway, the operation was advertised as "Toad River Lodge." The two brothers and their wives united forces till 1952, when Lash and Winnie sold their interest and moved a bit south to ranch at Mile 419 on the Racing River. Dennis and Marj sold the lodge to new owners in 1966. Their daughters Gloria and Janice, and their nephews, were schooled in Fort Nelson, staying with relatives. All their children have tales to tell of having to go to school far away, and not seeing their parents.[50]

---

[50] Their experience, of course, paled in comparison to that of Indigenous people in the same era, who endured residential schools which not only removed their children from parents and community, but actively worked to suppress native languages and cultures. Children were subjected to physical and sexual abuse, hard labour, and starvation; family transmission of culture and knowledge was broken, causing damage to subsequent generations as well. A Canadian government apology for the destructive process of residential schools was made in 2008. "For more than a century, Indian Residential Schools separated over 150,000 Aboriginal children from their families and communities. In the 1870's, the federal government, partly in order to meet its obligation to educate Aboriginal children, began to play a role in the development and administration of these schools. Two primary objectives of the Residential Schools system were to remove and isolate children from the influence of their homes, families, traditions and cultures, and to assimilate them into the dominant culture. These objectives were based on the assumption Aboriginal cultures and spiritual beliefs were inferior and unequal. Indeed, some sought, as it was infamously said, 'to kill the Indian in the child.' Today, we recognize that this policy of assimilation was wrong, has caused great harm, and has no place in our country." Stephen Harper, Prime Minister of Canada, June 11, 2008, from the *Statement of Apology*.

Dennis used to keep a spotting telescope at the Toad River Lodge. You didn't have to be a hunter to look up to the mountains and hills across the river and see Stone Sheep grazing. In the winter, the valley, which was burnt off every spring to encourage the growth of pasture grasses for the horses, provided good wintering for the sheep.

Classic postcard image of the Toad River Lodge in the 1950s.

At Mile 710, just over the border in the Yukon Territory, lies another Highway lodge associated with the Callison family, also one of the original highway lodges. Rancheria Lodge was built after the war by the British Yukon Navigation Company, a subsidiary of the White Pass and Yukon Railway. This company had a monopoly on travel corridors in the Yukon at the time, and in 1946 they started a bus route over the Alaska Highway from Dawson Creek to Whitehorse. They built four lodges along the way to serve as gas stations and refreshment stops for their buses.[51] William (Bud) Simpson, husband of John's sister Doris, helped build the first hotel out of logs, and when the people contracted to run the lodge backed out, Bud and Doris put a down payment on it and opened it. They ran it for 28 years, selling gas, serving meals, and making beds, gradually enlarging the lodge and restaurant with lumber from abandoned highway camps in the area. The 1950 edition of the AAA guide *Alaska and the Alaska Highway* listed the Rancheria this way: "*Hotel, 13 rooms, 4 baths. Single $1.25 to $2.50, double $3 to $4. Very plain rooms but a better than average meal stop for this area.*" A few years later, in 1959, in a Canadian government Travel Bureau pamphlet, *Alaska Highway, Road to Yukon Adventure*, the lodge advertised: *Accom., meals, gas*

---

[51] http://sightsandsites.ca/south/site/rancheria-lodge

& oil, car storage, minor car repairs, tires, store, fishing boat rental, guide service. Accommodates 34 people.

Today many visitors come in RVs, but in the 1940s, it was these modern buses that brought tourists to Alaska!

Weather along the highway was subject to abrupt change. Fierce snowstorms, arriving unexpectedly over the mountains, could block the roads. In such bad weather, the Rancheria—like the Toad River Lodge—was a welcome sight and would shelter everyone who stopped, even if it meant that people had to share single beds, or sleep on barstools or under the restaurant tables. It all made travel rather adventurous! Doris was famed for being able to keep everyone fed under adverse conditions for days.

In the mid 1970s, the Simpsons added a cocktail lounge, beer parlour, and motel rooms. They had to keep up with the times! The lodge is still open today under other owners, and offers RV parking as well as rooms, gas, repairs, and meals.

The first highway was barely passable, and it was easy to get stuck in the gumbo. It took many years to upgrade and develop into the modern highway it is today. The Canadian section of the Alaska Highway was fully paved in 1992, and had been widened and straightened. Today over 300,000 tourists take to the highway annually:

the trip of a lifetime! Many of the old lodges are still open to guests; others are closed now but the buildings are still there, like small ghost towns, testifying to the great age of lodges and automobiles, an age of optimism and adventure in which the Callisons played a big role.

VIGNETTE: Not Just on the Ground, but In The Air!

John's brother Pat Callison had a powerful part in Northern development as well, working from the air to support the building of the Canol Road in the Yukon during the war.

Prior to that, in the late 1930s, he'd gone to Dease Lake with his father Fred and his own young family, leaving the Montney Valley and his siblings for new horizons. Pat and his wife Ethel owned and operated the Lakeview Roadhouse on the south end of Dease Lake from 1938 to 1941, and Pat bought a truck and trucked supplies between Telegraph Creek and Dease Lake. In 1939, he bought a one-third interest in a Curtis Robin aircraft, took flying lessons in Vancouver for two winters, and started Cassiar Airways.

As the Yukon Transportation Museum recounts: "Pat started his flying career in 1939 at Dease Lake, B.C. He flew for Northern Airways from 1942 until 1947, when he and his family moved to Dawson City and started Callison's Flying Services. In 1955 he sold the fixed-wing operation and formed Klondike Helicopters, the first Yukon-based helicopter company. Pat chronicled his life pioneering transportation in the North in his own book, "Pack Dogs to Helicopters."[52]

The coming of aviation to the Yukon was soon to mean the end of working dogteams in the area. Planes flown by Pat Callison and others could easily land on any of the numerous bodies of water or on ice, and helicopters could land anywhere. Servicing riverboats, mining operations, and other sites was easier and cheaper from the air.

Pat and Ethel Callison had two daughters: Joan and Fay. Pat later retired to the balmier temperatures of the West Coast, but returned frequently to the north, flying his own plane to visit his daughter and his grandchildren, who were gleeful at being able to fly with him on a whim to pay visits!

---

[52]http://www.virtualmuseum.ca/sgc-cms/histoires_de_chez_nous-community_memories/pm_v2.php?id=story_line&lg=English&fl=0&ex=00000377&sl=4624&pos=1

It Grows on the Land
Recipes and Cures

One of the most time-consuming jobs for a woman on a homestead or in the bush was the growing, preparation, and preservation of food. Cabins did not have electricity, so there were no refrigerators apart from those using ice, so food had to be dried, smoked, cured in brine, or vacuum-packed in jars—a process called "canning." Alone on traplines, men didn't can meat, generally, and drying was the principal method of preservation. As well, venison and moose could be kept frozen during the coldest winter simply by hanging it outside in a raised cache out of reach of predators. Women took pride in being able to can almost anywhere. Out on a fishing trip of several days with John and her nephew Bill in the 1970s, when she was in her sixties, Anne canned their catch of trout on the Coleman gas camping stove! The last couple of days' catch were brought home fresh to freeze at home.

In honour of my own childhood in Calgary, thriving all winter on moosemeat and venison canned or frozen by Anne Callison and served up by my mother in various forms—stew, sukiyaki, chili, spaghetti sauce, meatloaf, sloppy joes, tacos, and porcupines—and in memory of the vast women's enterprise of canning, it's only fitting to include instructions for canning meat. It's a practice still common in some rural areas, where the rich taste and tenderness of canned meat is appreciated by all.

VIGNETTE Canned Moosemeat (Venison, Elk, Bear)

- Boil jars and lids 10 min to sterilize. Cut meat in 1" cubes; pack in jars up to the bottom of the neck, fairly tightly. Add 1 tsp canning (non iodized) salt, and 1 tbsp water on top. Wipe jar rims clean. Seal jars finger-tight only.

- Old method (not recommended for meat!): Place jars in rack and fill canning pot with water to the top of the necks of the jars. Bring to a boil, then reduce the heat and gently simmer 4 hrs. Or (recommended for meat) use a pressure cooker-canner, with 2" water in the bottom, at 10 lb pressure for 75 min to can pints and 90 min for quarts (at elevations higher than 1000 ft, use higher pressure, up to 15 lb). Make sure jars do not touch.

- Remove jars from the water using tongs, and let cool. Within 10-15 min you'll hear a "pop" as lids seal. Check each lid to make sure it is sealed (sealed lids do not move). If jars do not seal, refrigerate and use in the next couple of days.

- Keep jars in a cool place. Meat is cooked and just needs reheating to the simmering point afterward. Add to sautéed vegetables and simmer to make a stew, or chop the meat smaller to make spaghetti sauce or chili con carne. Heat and slice to make hot meat sandwiches.

I can already hear the "pop!" of opening a jar, releasing the vacuum!

In gardens in the summer, people grew root vegetables like potatoes, turnips, carrots, parsnips, and onions, which could be kept in root cellars through winter, along with cabbages (though they tend to go black on the outside, and pale and bitter on the inside and thus can't be kept as long). Cabbages would also be prepared in barrels in brine (sauerkraut). Tomatoes, green and yellow beans, some of the onions, shelled peas, and tomatoes, green as well as ripe, would be canned on the farm before heading out to the trapline. Lettuces, radishes, tomatoes, and parsley were grown for use in the summer, and dill to use fresh or dried. And every household had one or more rhubarb plants!

In the wild, there were saskatoons (called service berries in Eastern Canada by those who did not learn of them from the Cree), raspberries, strawberries, huckleberries, cranberries, blueberries in late summer and early fall. These were canned as jams, compotes, or, in thicker form, as pie filling. Other plants were used from the forest as well: birch trees were tapped for syrup and sugar-making in spring, garlic and horseradish were gathered wild in late summer, garlic shoots in late spring.[53]

---

[53] I remember my mother and a neighbour canning garden vegetables in 1957 in Calgary (in 1958 after Bill arrived, we got a freezer, and canning stopped). Long green beans, yellow beans, and shucked peas were the favourites as unlike carrots, parsnips, and potatoes, these vegetables would not survive in our basement cold room all winter. Auntie Anne sent us cases of canned moosemeat and venison by Greyhound, and later, huge chunks of frozen moosemeat, wrapped in newspaper and packed in cardboard boxes with dry ice. We'd go to the bus station in Calgary and retrieve the boxes. At times the ice still steamed! My mother would take a chunk of meat out of the freezer, leave it for a few hours, cut off what had thawed until there was enough for dinner, then return the rest to the freezer. I remember big salamis as well. Even later on, when my Mom stopped growing a big garden (she started work and there was more money for food), we still grew rhubarb, lettuce, carrots, parsley, dill. We picked saskatoons every year on the banks of the Glenmore Reservoir at the Weaselhead, on the city side (the other side was the Tsuu Tina Reserve). We also picked saskatoons on Saskatoon Mountain, when we visited the Grendys homestead, which was Uncle Joe's farm when I was small.

Cures usually involved ingredients common in the kitchen or forest, and were used to treat common ailments. Over-the-counter salves such as Absorbine Jr. and Vick's Vaporub also played a role; an old clean sock soaked in Vick's and worn around the neck was a cure for sore throat and breathing difficulties, for example. Spruce tar was used as antiseptic on cuts and scratches; garlic was used for toothache and sore throat.

This is a home cure from Anne Callison's archive, not in her own handwriting but in someone else's, which includes ingredients rather exotic for the time: citrus fruit. Anne must have saved this cure at a time when John's hip "arthur-itis," as he called it, was really bothering him.

VIGNETTE: Home Cures

Help for Arthritis Relief
attributed to "Margaret Newkirk, Maple Creek SK" (poss. 1914-2004)
-Juice of 3 grapefruits, 3 lemons, 3 oranges
-Take one qt of boiling water and in it dissolve 2 dessert-spoons of cream of tartar, 2 tsp epson salts. Mix all together & take 4 oz every morning, one hour before breakfast.
-Drink 1 glass of water, after breakfast. Do not eat chocolate in any form. Do not eat white sugar to excess. Do eat coarse grain cereal, etc. You may not find much relief for about 2 weeks. But keep on this for 6 months. Return to it at the first sign of the Arthritis. Eat lots of tomatoes in any form.

As previously noted, Anne's skills at preserving, provisioning, cooking, and budgeting on farm and trapline served her in later years when she worked with the CWL women in Dawson Creek and Fort St. John, catering large banquets. I wanted to include two recipes from those days. The first is a memento of the 1960s American craze for "aspic" or cold jellied salads, filled with all kinds of chopped meat and vegetables, sometimes mixed together and sometimes prepared in spectacular layers of different colours. The photocopy in Anne's papers, from *News of the Northland* in September 1955, cuts off part of the recipe, so I offer another. The same newsletter proposes Shortribs Supreme, Sweet and Sour Cabbage—with bacon of course—and Butterscotch-Pecan Refrigerator Cakes made with powdered butterscotch pudding mix! The issue also included tips for buying an electric stove, and—it was hunting season—The Ten Commandments of Gun Safety. The second recipe here is for another jelled wonder, "Strawberry Delight."

The third, after a pause for a food memory, is for more modern palate: Anne's recipe for carrot cake from a handwritten note in one of her banquet notebooks. She must have multiplied it many times to serve everyone. (PS. None of the recipes come with guarantees!)

Ham Aspic

4 cups ham, chopped or ground
1 cup chopped celery
1 cup crushed soda crackers
1 cup mayonnaise
1 box gelatin dissolved in ½ cup cold water
3 chopped pimentos (tinned)
2 chopped green peppers
1 small onion, chopped
3 hard boiled eggs, roughly chopped
2 tsp. lemon juice

Mix all, add mayonnaise last. Pour into an interesting mould and chill overnight. Turn out on a plate lined with lettuce leaves. Serves 18-20 people as part of a buffet dinner.

Strawberry Delight

Crust
1½ cups graham wafer crumbs
½ cup brown sugar
½ cup butter

Mix and put on bottom of 9x13 pan, saving ½ cup for the top.

Topping
2 pkg Jello
2 cups boiling water
1 pkg frozen strawberries

Combine Jello and boiling water and stir till powder is dissolved. Mix in berries and let sit until just about set. Whip 2 pkg dream whip and fold in. Pour over crust in pan. Sprinkle with remaining crumbs. Chill well till serving.

VIGNETTE: An Erín Food Memory

In this memory, Anne's sister Mary is in the Tom Baker Cancer Centre in Calgary, in her last prolonged bout with the disease from which she died in January, 2007. Anne wanted to visit her; Mary wanted no visit. Anne fumed and insisted. Finally, she came regardless, down from Fort St. John to NW Calgary, driven by her trusty grandson Clinton. She brought jars and jars of homemade rhubarb juice to her sister. Who knows what it was meant to cure! But Mary was glad she came.

Anne Callison's Carrot Cake

1½ cup melted oil, or 1 c melted margarine, or ½ c marg and ½ c oil
2 cups   white sugar
4 eggs   added one at a time and beaten well
2 cups   grated carrots
2 cups   flour
1 tsp   soda
1 tsp   baking powder
1 tsp   cinnamon
¼ tsp   salt
9 x 13   pan

Mix together 3 tbsp brown sugar and 1 tsp cinnamon and sprinkle on cake as a topping, before baking. Bake at 350ºF for 40-45 min. Serve w. whip cream. [Note! Not tested! And.... an alarming amount of sugar!]

An early photo of Anne cooking: she's in slacks and dark blouse, helping prepare lunch for a group on a day out at the Wapiti River in Alberta, in the summer of 1942. The women are both working; one of the fellows is doing the manly job of minding the fire, and the other, well, it looks like he just might be taking a snooze!

Dec 14th Banquet
155 people

4   Turkeys
2   hams   2 left over from Dec 13
30 lb potatoes   30 lb left
30   peas & carrots   4 "
15 hd lettuce
5 lb   Butter
10 14oz Cranberries
1 jar   Salad dressing
13 dozen buns
1 lb   tea
4 "   coffee   coffee stored night
6   sugar
2 gt   milk
15 / 2 gl ice cream
10   strawberries
16   candles   (Grocers came to)
       Radishes   ($175.42)
       muffins
       tomatoes

Banquet shopping list, handwritten by Anne in one of her CWL notebooks. 155
people, total cost for groceries: $175.42! This would have been in the early 1970s.
It reminds me of all the family dinners Anne used to cook at the drop of a hat
when she came to visit, unless my mother managed to stop her!

Bannock

The Relation Between Indigenous and Settler Peoples

Bannock was and is a staple of life on the land and on the trapline. Before flour came with the fur trade, a cake-like bread was made with starchy roots such as cattail. Dry it, pound it, mix it with bear fat and dried berries. Yes, it's the ancestor to the modern energy bar! When Indigenous people first started using wheat flour in the fur trade era, they ate bannock only when moosemeat was short. Bannock became more common as game receded, and as the demands to feed the occupants of forts brought meat shortages. Bannock can be oven-baked, pan-fried, deep-fried, or fire-cooked in a pan or wrapped around a stick. It can be made into loaves, or spoon-dropped in hot oil. Some people put raisins in it, berries dried or fresh, sugar, and eat it with butter and jam, or with cheez-whiz, or make it into sandwiches.

The presence of this bread on traplines and tote roads, around campfires and in tents and teepees, is a memory sign of the first links between Indigenous and white peoples, between people of the land and newcomers. Not an easy relationship, but in the early bush days experienced by John and Anne Callison, it was a relationship of respectful difference. In honour of the shared love of cooking, bannock here has its own chapter. I see it as a symbol of recovery, not of *reconciliation* as an empty word but as a process of rethinking, listening, renegotiation, and renewal, now begun but still lying in the future.

VIGNETTE: *People to People, Nation to Nation: Report of the Royal Commission on Aboriginal People (1996)*

"The relationship between Aboriginal and non-aboriginal people evolved through 4 stages:
1. Pre-contact - Aboriginal and non-Aboriginal people lived on separate continents and knew nothing of one another.
2. Years following first contact - fragile relations of peace, friendship and rough equality.
3. Power shifted to non-Aboriginal people and governments. They moved Aboriginal people off most of their lands and took steps to "civilize" them by teaching them European ways.
4. Presently, it is a time for recovery for Aboriginal people and culture, a time for critical review of our relationship, and time for its renegotiation and renewal."

In hope of a better future, and out of respect for all those who shared recipes and food, even when relations were understandably uneasy, here are a few bannock recipes, of different styles, amalgams of a hundred recipes. If the ingredients aren't exact, it doesn't seem to matter. Bannock is forgiving! You just have to learn to make it on your particular stove or wood fire, with your flour, the fat you have on hand, at the altitude where you find you are hungry. Remember, as you cook, the philosophy of Anne's sister Mary, which is almost a grace: "Eat food with humility: it teaches us meaning."

Bannock Oven Loaf

4 cups flour
1.5 tbsp baking powder
¼ tsp salt
¼ tsp sugar
3 tbsp shortening
1½ - 2 cups warm water

Preheat oven to 350-400°F. Mix dry ingredients thoroughly then add water. Knead a few times gently. Spread dough over a greased cookie sheet. Pierce with fork here and there and bake till done, about 20 minutes.

Drop-Style Fried Bannock

4 c. flour
2 tbsp. baking powder
2 tbsp. sugar
1 tsp. salt
3 c. water
Raisins (optional)
Cooking fat of your choice, but bear fat if possible.

Combine all dry ingredients in a bowl. Add water, and raisins if desired, and mix batter until it is a dropping consistency. Melt cooking fat in frying pan until a few drops of water sizzle. Drop big tablespoons of batter into hot fat and fry till brown all over.
Add butter and jam if it appeals! Enjoy.

Bannock For Every Fire

2 cups flour
1 heaping tbsp lard or oil
1 tbsp sugar
1 tsp salt
1 tbsp baking powder
almost 1 cup water

Butter a 9-10" cast iron frying pan and heat slowly. Now mix dry ingredients in a bowl and then add water to make a stiff ball of dough. Knead a bit then pat into a flat bread more than 1" thick. **Cook in the pan** slowly over fire (or over medium heat on top of stove) till cooked through (about 20 min). If you like, you can turn it partway. You can also bake on a greased baking sheet in the oven at 350°F for 25-30 minutes. Also, dry ingredients can be mixed and bagged in advance and then just add water and oil when you go to cook it.

Trail Bannock for Two (pan or stick over the fire)

1 cup flour
1 tsp baking powder
¼ tsp salt
3 tbsp margarine or shortening or lard

Sift dry ingredients. Cut in fat until the mix has the texture of coarse sand (at this point, you can put it in a plastic bag and do the rest in the bush). When preparing your dinner, heat a greased frying pan. Add COLD water (bit less than ½ cup) to the dry mix, combining quickly to make a firm dough. Form dough into flat breads about ½" thick, and dust with flour. Lay bannocks in warm frying pan. Hold over heat, rotating pan a little. Once bottom crust has formed and dough is cooked enough to hold together, turn bannock. Cook 12-15 min. To cook on a stick, make a thicker dough by adding less water and roll dough into a long ribbon of max. 1" in diameter. Wind dough around a preheated green stick and cook 8" above flame; turn stick until bannock is done.

And did I mention *cattail*? Cattails are amazing plants. They have been a source of food and medicine, and of material for baskets, cords, mats, and ropes for thousands of years. They grow readily in wet soil and watery environments, such as muskeg, of which the North Peace

129

has plenty. The first tender shoots can be cut and sautéed in a pan and eaten. Later, when young cattail flowerheads appear, they can be boiled and eaten like corn on the cob, or pickled. In late summer, the pollen can be picked, ground, and added to other flours (higher protein). The roots can be mashed and dried, then ground into flour. They can be also be boiled and prepared like potatoes. Medicinal uses: both the pollen and the root are astringent, and help remove infection or stop bleeding; fresh pounded root or pollen mixed with honey can be used as a poultice on infections and blisters. Mashed root can be used as toothpaste. A marvel!

Two qualifiers: if their water is industrially contaminated by nearby lumber or mining or oil installations, the roots will absorb lead and mercury, and should not be eaten. Moose also eat cattail shoots and roots, so in some areas, moosemeat also may become contaminated. Also—if you are elsewhere in Canada as it has not yet reached the Peace River Country—be sure not to harvest the invasive species yellow iris by mistake, as it is toxic.[53]

---

[53] If you search on the internet for the keywords "moose," "oil sands," and "contamination," you will find the latest information. And check sites like http://www.invadingspecies.com/yellow-iris/ to help identify the right plant.

Murdale and Saskatoon Mountain
Update on the Homesteads

John was the Callison son who returned each year to the homestead in the Montney valley. He faithfully cleared land, planted crops, and minded the Callison horses. From 1936 on, he also cared for his mother, first at Murdale and then in Dawson Creek until her death in 1945.

Back in the spring of 1936, John had travelled to Vancouver with his furs, thinking to get a better price by selling directly to Pappas Furs there. His younger brother and sister, twins Dennis and Daisy, had been in Vancouver going to school since the year before, living with their mother in a rented house at Gilmore and Venables Street. When he left Vancouver, Daisy went back with him, to get out of a Depression era job working in Kresge's under terrible conditions for paltry pay. On their long and winding bus trip north through Alberta, they witnessed the terrible Dust Bowl effects on the prairie when they were caught in a dust storm. Definitely life was better in the green North!

The school year over, Dora Callison made the decision to return from Vancouver and live at Murdale instead of rejoining Fred, who had moved further north to the Cassiar area of B.C., north of Dease Lake. Fred Callison had mining claims there, and a horse ranch nearby that he wanted to develop. He later had a second family in his new life there.[54]

Dora Callison kept house for John at the Murdale homestead, and lived with Mollie, her youngest, while Mollie went to the local school. When Mollie reached high school age, John purchased his mother's share of the ranch, which enabled her to move with Mollie to Dawson Creek and buy a house there.[55]

Gradually, John bought up quarter-sections adjoining the original four staked by Fred, John, Pat, and Lynch, when they came up for sale in the years after the war. People in the area were moving out in the

---

[54] With his partner Ethel Quock, member of the Tahltan Nation at Telegraph Creek whom he married after the death of Dora, Fred had seven children. Four lived to adulthood: Dempsey (a famed guide—http://tahltan.ca/wp-content/uploads/2014/04/Interior-News-Article-on-Dempsey.pdf), Jerry, Annie, and Sam.
[55] Info in the first four paragraphs is derived from *Mountain Trails*, 186-188.

great Canadian postwar urbanization—so many soldiers did not want to return to the harsh life of the homesteads and had other ambitions. John loved the land he lived on, and didn't want it to fall into the hands of people who wouldn't work it and care for it. He ended up with twelve quarter-sections, or three sections, a considerable ranch.

Anne recalls that the family economy after the war still ran on very little cash. After making a deal to buy one quarter, John valiantly paid up all the back taxes owed on the land from the Depression years, a situation that was very common. Months later, he received a letter from the government saying he still owed 30 cents. After several notices came, Anne wrote back asking if they would add the 30 cents to the next year's taxes instead, as if they kept insisting, the Callisons would have to sell this new quarter to come up with the 30 cents. Anne always wished she'd kept the government correspondence and had it framed!

As did other farmers and ranchers, John employed Indigenous workers in the summer to help with the backbreaking labour of haying. At fall harvest as well, they'd hire on to help with the cutting, stooking, gathering stooks, hauling them on horse-drawn wagons, and throwing bundles into threshers—a process entirely automated and done by one machine today. There are stories that John would bail out young Indigenous guys who'd ended up in jail in Fort St. John for falling afoul of city ordinances. He would bring them home to Montney and sit them down in the kitchen, asking Anne to give them coffee, lots of coffee. They'd sit with Anne and tell tales, sip and doze, till they were ready to go to work or head home. It was John's way of breaking them out of the harms of the system, while acting like he was part of the system, I think. He acted as best he could as a kind of porous barrier between newcomer law and order, and traditional cycles of Indigenous life.

Murdale was still a part-time residence; John and Anne took care of the growing and harvesting there, but spent winters in Dawson Creek running the motel and raising their boys. At times, they rented the land to others to farm, when they were not able to attend to it.

Meanwhile, after the war, by 1949 or so, the Montney reservation was no longer, and the Dane-zaa people for the most part lived further away. Even so, they continued to hunt and move all across their traditional areas up through the 1960s, as much "Crown" land was still undeveloped. The surge in the oil industry—predicted even back at the time of Treaty 8—was the next incursion that created change.

One of the main postwar events at the Murdale homestead was the coming of the railway. The Fort Nelson Subdivision was built in the 1960s by the Pacific Great Eastern Railway from Fort St. John to Fort Nelson, completing a line that went from Vancouver to Prince George, then to Fort St. John. The subdivision opened in 1971, and the next year the company became BC Rail. In 2004, BC Rail was leased to CN Rail for 999 years. At time of writing in 2017, there was only one train per week in each direction between Fort St. John and Fort Nelson.

The PGE had arrived in 1958 in Fort St. John, linking with the railhead of Northern Alberta Railways, which followed a geographically more natural route southeast into Alberta. Surveying then commenced between Fort St. John and Fort Nelson, 400 km distant, and farmland was expropriated for the line. The surveyors, in passing through the Montney Valley, apparently used the Callison homestead house, left unlocked, as their bunkhouse. The rail line passed just to the rear of the house, as a lot of it was surveyed over the Old Fort Nelson Trail. No one knows how, and no one took responsibility, but one day in the late 50s or early 60s, the house burned to the ground. "A fire set on the floor?" wonders her son Wayne. "Careless smoking," surmises Anne.

As the builders of the line passed through the homestead, they struck a spring behind the house that had channelled water underground to Montney Creek. Today, that spring provides the new house with water.

Another big change came with the advent of the automobile and the highway as the main means of transport, leaving horses and dogs for bush activities alone. People often still travelled together in convoys, though, in case one vehicle got stuck in the famous Peace River gumbo, otherwise known as mud!

Callisons near Fort Nelson in the late 40s. John at right; Anne between vehicles.

Time also brought changes on Saskatoon Mountain, at the Grendys homestead where Anne had grown up. Both Anne's parents became citizens before the war. It was as "Anastazyja Grendysz" of "Wembley Alberta" that Anne's mother, recorded as being from Poland (which it still was at the time) became a Canadian citizen on June 3, 1938, in category A, that of married women whose husbands were already citizens. "Thomas Grendysz," along with "Anna, Mary, and Joe," had become naturalized Canadians on March 17.[57]

Mary, who spent time at the farm during the war, seldom spoke of those years (she was recovering from illness) but recalled her parents whispering at night of letters received from the Old Country, detailing genocide in and near their village, a zone occupied by the Nazi General Government. The Jewish population was murdered by 1943; as the village was on the rail line to Lviv, villagers would have witnessed closed trains sent north in 1942 that never returned,[58] and would have known of mass shootings of Jews at Bobrka. Ukrainians and Poles were then set against each other; finally the war ended with Soviet annexation, and banishment of any remaining people identified as Poles to Poland, and others to Siberia. In Alberta, no more letters arrived after the war.

Both Joe and Leo served in Canada's army (Leo became a citizen in

---

[57] *The Canada Gazette* for June 1938, page 854 and June 18, 1938, page 3219.
[58] Their destination was the Belzec death camp, which only 7 people survived.

1946, along with his first daughter Nellie, who died soon after).[59] Leo went overseas and fought in the liberation of Holland, probably participating in the Scheldt Estuary battles that helped free the Dutch from Nazi rule but with brutal effect on the Canadians. Leo returned shell-shocked; it was a family tragedy. His Dutch wife Trudy (Gertrude) came back to Canada with him, and they had a family together, but Leo often lived like a hermit. Although Joe watched over the family, Trudy took the brunt of the responsibility. "It was sad," says Anne, "but in those days you served; you did what you were told; you did your duty."[60]

Trudy Grendys holding Fred, with Klaas, Peter, Gary and the younger Nellie, 1956.

---

[59] Because John, Pat, Lynch, and Dennis were working on the Alcan Highway and Canol Road, considered critical defense projects, the government agreed to only call them up in an emergency.

[60] Joe told me stories of the war, in 2005. He said Leo wrote him from overseas telling him that the war was terrible and advising him to do anything possible to avoid being sent into action. "Shoot yourself in the foot," Leo apparently urged. Joe, as it turned out, fell from a cliff during commando training and incurred a shoulder injury that affected him all his life. He was not sent into action.

On July 9, 1947, after demobilization, Joe had married Kathleen Carter at a wedding of four couples that included Vella Carter, Kathleen's sister. Joe and Kathleen later had two children, Shona and Brent, who grew up on the farm and in Grande Prairie where they later went to school.

Anne's parents gradually retired in the 1950s, and moved to a small house with a huge garden on the flood plain of Bear Creek in Grande Prairie. Joe, after the war, ably took over the farming. As well, he took on a lot of family responsibility, looking out for his older brother Leo, giving him work when Leo was healthy enough, and helping to look out for Leo's family. Meanwhile, older brother Alex, who lived in New York state, looked out for Leo's twin John until John returned to Canada; as well, he raised his own daughter Sharon Alexis with his wife Sophie.

Leo's family lived on a quarter section near the Grendys farm, and Trudy Grendys created a very neat-as-a-pin home for their brood: Peter, Klaas, Nellie, Gary, and Fred. The stresses were many, though. Joe, Anne, and Mary fretted and sorrowed at times. It was rumoured that Trudy wanted to return to Holland at some point, but she did end up staying. I remember visiting my cousins at their house just once, and was impressed with how everything and everyone fit so neatly into a small space. Another amazement that stayed with me was that they assembled picture puzzles, then glued them to board and hung them on the walls! I spent some time very enthused by the creativity of this idea.

Farming on Saskatoon Mountain being marginal at best, Joe also worked at the American military installation atop Saskatoon Mountain. It opened in 1953 as one of a line of surveillance stations with radar domes (radomes) on the Pinetree Line of NORAD, North America's air defense against Russian missiles during the Cold War. The base on Saskatoon Mountain was run by the USAF 919th Aircraft Control and Warning Squadron until 1963 and then by the Canadian RCAF 57th Control and Warning Squadron until it was decommissioned in 1988.[61] Joe's American dual citizenship was a help in his obtaining work with the Americans. Joe was also active in the farming community and in the National Farmers' Union, and worked the farm until he retired.

---

[61] With the last buildings gone, in 1995 this grassy site in the boreal forest, once Dane-zaa berry picking and plant gathering land, became the Saskatoon Mountain Natural Area, open for day use by hikers, cross-country skiers, ATV users, picnickers, berry pickers, "primitive" hunters, horseback riders.

Joe Grendys on his wedding day, second from left, with his bride Kathleen in front of him. Her sister Vella is at left of photo; she became Vella Brownschlaigle (d. 1979).

The homestead quarter where the Grendys house stands is no longer farmed, though part of what was the larger farm is. The last time I was there with my brother Bill, after our Uncle Joe's death in 2005, the family of an oilfield worker lived in the house; for them it was a rural acreage. Before our arrival, they had just torn down and hauled away the old barn. The era of the homestead was definitely over.

1960s, Anne's four brothers: Leo and John behind, Joe and Alex in front.

Grandparents Tom and Anastazyja Grendys with Joe and Kathleen's children Shona and Brent at Christmas, 1958.

The Coming of Change
Big Dams on the Peace, and Oil Underneath

When asked on video in 2007 in an interview about changes she'd seen in the North Peace, Anne's first reply was "oh my goodness!" The changes were so many, it was hard to know where to start!

The biggest changes that affected people were personal, those that not only indicated an alteration in the landscape, but left individuals with an altered sense of place. Anne recalls that for her, this was being unable to keep their home open to anyone who came by. Doors had to be locked, particularly after their home at Murdale was lost to fire.

Oil and gas exploration—long predicted by the Dane-zaa dreamers such as Charlie Yahey and foreseen by the Federal government even before Treaty 8—was one of the greatest changes after the Alaska Highway came. Exploration was carried out on the Callison farmlands at Murdale but, Anne says, the crews cleaned up after drilling. Today on those fields in the Montney Valley, there's no sign of industry apart from the rail track and weekly freight train from Fort St. John to Fort Nelson.

For the rest of the world outside the North Peace, however, the word "Montney" has taken on new meaning. The name of the Dane-zaa chief Muckethay which for years had designated a creek, its beautiful valley, and the hub of a community of newcomers north of Fort St. John and Charlie Lake refers, since 1962 and the drilling of Texaco's Buick Creek No. 7 well, to a vast area under the earth, the "Montney Formation."[59] Its siltstone, shale, and sand extend from Fort Nelson in B.C. down into Alberta; they hold reserves of 449 trillion cubic feet of natural gas, almost 15,000 million barrels of NGLs or "natural gas liquids,"[60] and 1,125 million barrels of oil, according to an industry study of 2013.[61] It was said in 2012 that the fossil fuel reserves of the Montney

---

[59] https://en.wikipedia.org/wiki/Montney_Formation

[60] Fossil fuel products difficult to remove from rock; they require "well stimulation" by hydraulic fracturing, "fracking," in which water, sand, and chemicals are injected at high pressure into rock layers to break them down and create conduits for removal of oil or gas.

[61] Joint report of the National Energy Board, BC Oil and Gas Commission and the Alberta Energy Regulator, 2013.

Formation could fuel all of Canada's oil needs for 145 years, at 2012 rates of consumption. The ongoing exploitation of the underground formation for oil and gas—through hydraulic fracturing of the underground rock to squeeze out the fossil fuels—is known in the oil industry and beyond as the "Montney Play." As the Dane-zaa had long predicted, the white man came to drill and extract "the grease of the giant animals" from beneath the surface of the earth.[62]

A quick look at charts and maps in *The Peace Region Atlas 2012* shows how the number of new wells has mushroomed since 1950, and leaves no doubt regarding the increasing presence of industrial activity, and disturbance of traditional Dane-zaa and Tsek'ene territories:

Year	# Wells	Annual rate of new wells
1950	15	
1970	2,328	
1950-1970		110
1990	5,425	
1970-1990		147
2011	16,267	
1990-2011		493

Oil and gas wells: number and annual rate of new wells[63]

First, there was the Alaska Highway, then all the roads from seismic exploration for oil, logging, and mining. Those activities brought people and prosperity to towns. But the roads gave access not just to extractive resources but also to the bush, and to people who otherwise could not have survived on their own in uncharted territory. This activity has only increased in intensity, raising grave concerns. "Since the release of the *2012 Atlas*, thousands more oil and gas activities have been authorized and thousands more hectares of forest have been cut in the region. In 2015, the Blueberry River First Nation filed a civil claim against the province of B.C. asserting that the scale and rate of industrial disturbances to the landscape authorized by the provincial government

---

[62] *The Place Where Happiness Dwells.* 143.

[63] Lee, P and M. Hanneman. *Atlas of land cover, industrial land uses and industrial-caused land change in the Peace Region of British Columbia.* Edmonton: Global Forest Watch Canada report #4, 2012, 63.

has gone too far.... The claim asserts that members no longer have access to sufficient land and resources in an uncontaminated state to sustain the patterns of economic activity, land use and occupation essential to their livelihood."[64]

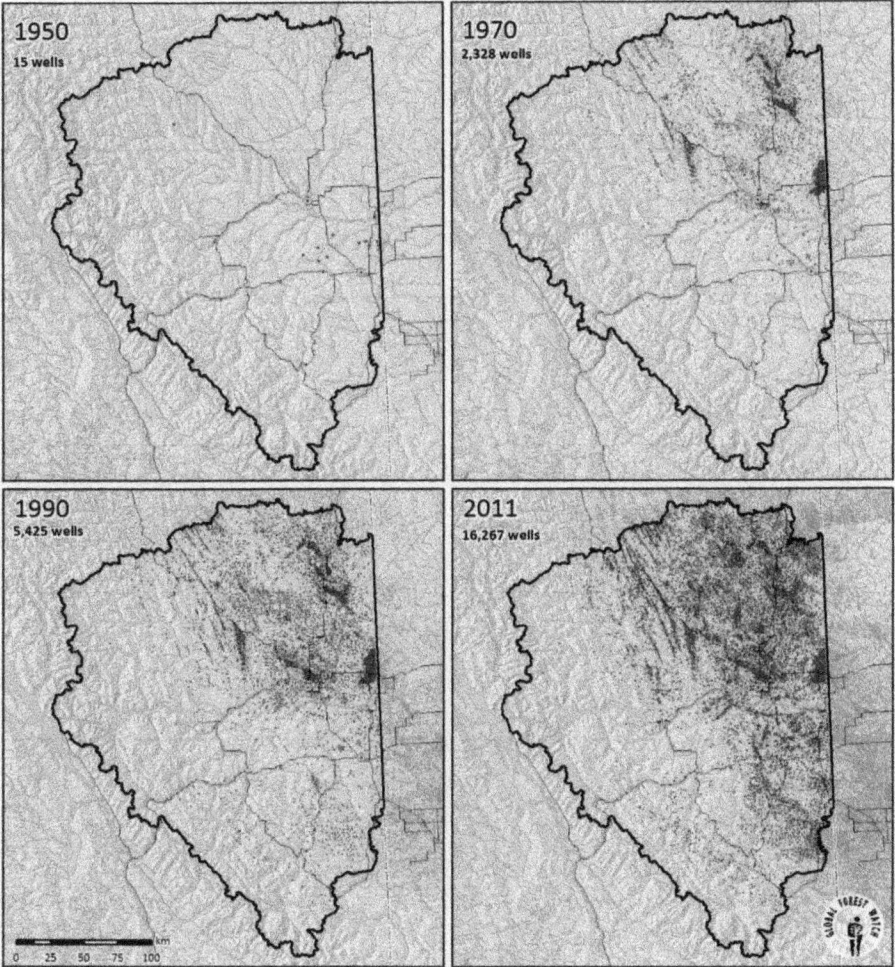

The growing black cloud shows the number of petroleum & natural gas wells in 1950, 1970, 1990, and 2011 in the Peace region of BC.[65] *See larger area on p. 142.*

See larger area on p. 142.

---

[64] Eliana Macdonald. *Atlas of Cumulative Landscape Disturbance in the Traditional Territory of the Blueberry River First Nations 2016.* Ecotrust Canada and David Suzuki Foundation, June 2016. 6.

[65] P. Lee and M. Hanneman. *Atlas of land cover, etc.* 65.

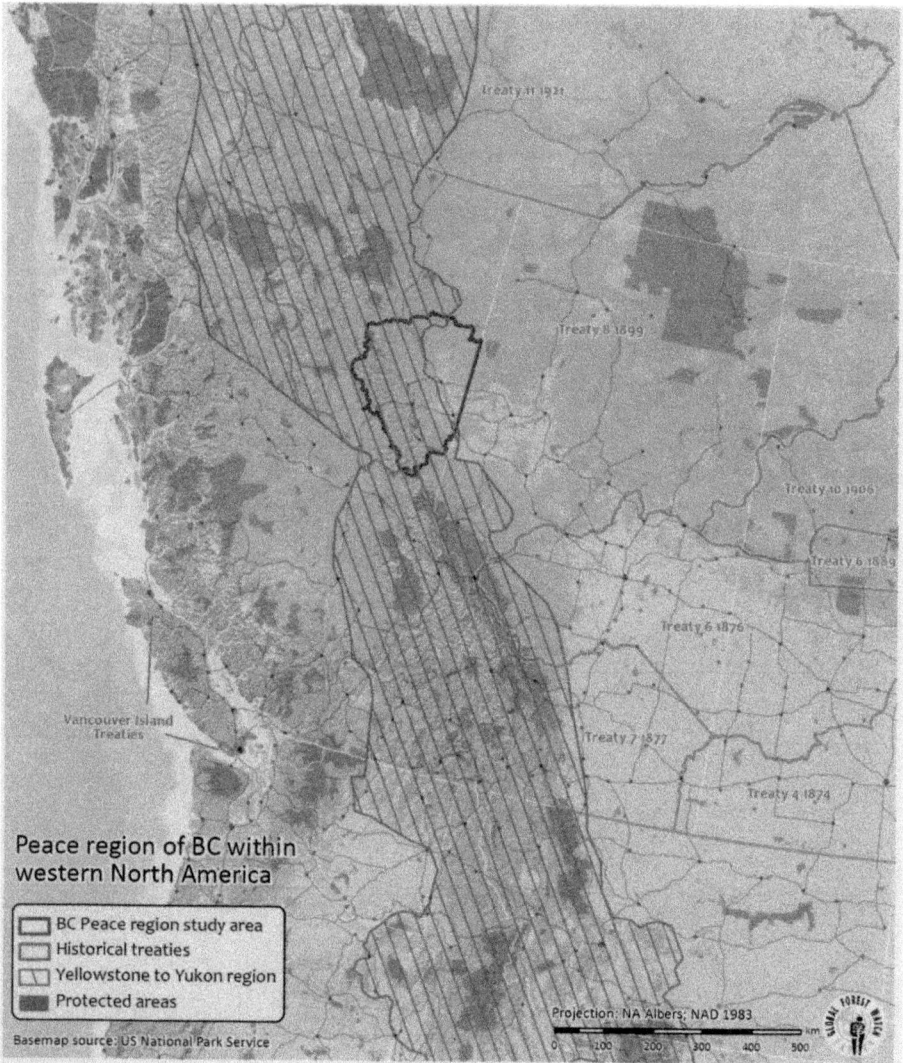

Peace Region of B.C. in western Canada. Area outlined in black is from the maps of wells on the previous page.[66]

The big dams on the Peace River were another major change to the North Peace in the era after the Alaska Highway, part of the great turn in Canada toward generation of hydro-electric power in the provinces with fast-running rivers: BC, Manitoba, Ontario, Newfoundland, and Quebec primarily. Hydro power has long been seen as "clean" power, and though it is cleaner than coal-fired generation, today not everybody

---

[66] P. Lee and M. Hanneman. *Atlas of land cover, etc.* 12.

considers it to be as ecological as solar power, for example. "Hydroelectric dams result in the generation of huge amounts of methane gas, a greenhouse gas, approximately 40 times more potent than carbon dioxide over 100 years, as these dams result in the flooding of large tracts of fertile land."[67] Levels of arsenic and mercury rise as well in the waters of the reservoirs, part of the accelerated processes of geological change from flooding lands formerly forest and valley. These chemicals contaminate fish too, rendering them less than safe for humans. Habitat fragmentation is increased by dams, and downstream river ecosystems are altered. Those in favour of hydro power feel the negative effects can be largely mitigated (by cutting and removing forests before flooding, for example), and that future needs for non carbon-based electricity generation make hydro power necessary. The public continues to weigh the merits and hazards of both views.

It only became economical in the 20th century to generate power so far from where it was primarily used, with the advent of new technologies for transmission lines. The first great dam, the W.A.C. Bennett Dam, was constructed on the Peace River between 1961-1968, 22 km west of Hudson Hope. It is one of the highest earth-filled dams on the planet. Its reservoir, Williston Lake, is 250 km long and has a surface area of over 1700 km^2—the largest man-made lake in North America and seventh largest in the world. Assembly places, hunting and berry picking sites, burial and sacred sites, and deer and moose calving places were engulfed by the rising waters; animal migration routes and human trails were erased as 350,000 acres of forest were flooded. First Nations communities were separated, and traditional river boats, wide and flat-bottomed, that once hauled freight and furs and people, were not safe on the open waters of the lake. The Peace River, first highway of the Peace Region, was now a barrier to navigation. Adjustments are still ongoing in Indigenous communities, as even BC Hydro recognizes.[68] In return, it was the province's booming population in the southwest that reaped the benefits of a cheap source of electric power for its industrial dreams.

As far as the great power dams on the Peace River were concerned, Anne Callison felt that they were a good thing, as they provide jobs, lake

---

[67] *Open Letter on the Health Impacts of the Site C Dam*, Dec. 4, 2017, by the BC members of the Canadian Association of Physicians for the Environment.
[68] Jonny Wakefield. "For Kwadacha First Nation, healing from W.A.C. Bennett Dam a work in progress." *Dawson Creek Mirror*, June 13, 2016.

waters for fishing and camping, and entice tourists seeking "wilderness" experiences. Anne's view, expressed in the pioneer video interview in 2007, was that of most white settlers in the region. The interviewer never asked about how these changes may have affected their Indigenous neighbours who had not given up their rights to fish and hunt, and earn their livelihoods on the affected lands.

Today, although it's far from universal, opinions are beginning to change. There is a call to recognize the cost of development to the lives of Indigenous people and to the landscape and the animals of the region, in the hope that better arrangements can be negotiated and agreement obtained *before* projects start. Benefits, as well, need to be shared equitably by all parties. An Open Letter on the Health Impacts of the Site C Dam, published December 4, 2017 by the BC members of the Canadian Association of Physicians for the Environment, summed up some of the current concerns regarding the North Peace:

> Studies from UNBC and SFU have identified that the cumulative effects of intense industrial development, including "two large-scale hydroelectric dams, 11 mines (gold-copper, coal), 8,000 oil and gas well sites, eight wind farms, various support facilities, 10,000 pipelines, numerous power lines, and smaller uses such as agriculture and guide-outfitting" erode Indigenous rights, mental health and traditional ways of life and culture."[69]

At the same time, there is no denying that huge infrastructure construction projects have brought the hope for prosperity and development to areas isolated from other types of economic opportunity.

Back during the first age in the 1960s of construction west of Hudson Hope (the third oldest settler community in BC), even I—in Calgary as a child—felt both the horror and the hope at the upcoming flooding of the North Peace valley. We visited the river one last time before it was to be flooded. I could tell my mother's heart was sad; she understood progress as inevitable, but regretted the loss of the valley. The Callisons too felt both sides of the story of change, with heartache and well as anticipation. John Callison did become a partner in the new Peace Glen Hotel in Hudson Hope, a coal-mining centre at the crossroads of the highway south via Chetwynd with the highways east into Alberta and north into the Yukon, via Fort St. John. Some of its

---

[69] *Open Letter...* op.cit.

coal, said to be the best steam coal in the continent, now lies in seams beneath the waters of the reservoir, and some north and west of it, but the demand for coal—a polluting source of power—is not what it was.

With the construction of the dam and the upcoming flooding of the Peace valley west of Hudson's Hope, a new road was rapidly built east to Fort St. John. Anne remarked that "many a team and wagon became mired in the mud, which is famous in the Peace River Country, on the old trail that followed closer to the Peace River. During the 1960s when the Bennett Dam was under construction, the new road, further from the river, was much used even though it was famed for its 'Texas gravel' that ruptured tires and gas tanks."[70] With the dam built, the thousands of construction workers vanished back south, and the trickle of tourists who came were looking for campsites, not hotels. John soon sold his interest in the Peace Glen Hotel.

In 1980, a second dam, the Peace Canyon, was completed 23 km downstream of the first, with a smaller 12 km reservoir named Dinosaur Lake. In 2015, after decades of forecasting and years of disagreement and incomplete or failed negotiations with First Nations over treaty rights, the BC government approved the construction of the dam at Site C, which will flood 80 km of the Peace Valley immediately south and west of Fort St. John. The Site C reservoir will be just 2-3 times the current width of the river; its smaller size is possible because it relies on the higher Williston Lake for water storage.[71] The decision to build the dam was upheld after the BC provincial elections in 2017, though it is still being contested in the courts by the West Moberley and Prophet River First Nations as of this writing. "We've never said no to the production of energy," says West Moberly First Nations chief Roland Willson, "we've said 'let's protect the valley. It's the last piece of our backyard that's relatively untouched.'"[72]

That the North Peace's struggles with the politics of hydro power are more public than similar struggles in other provinces, such as Labrador and Manitoba, is perhaps due to the opening of the area by the

---

[70] from a typescript of a text in Anne's archives.

[71] "...Site C will re-use the same water flowing downstream from the two upstream facilities. This will enable Site C to generate approximately 35% of the energy produced at the W.A.C. Bennett Dam, with only 5% of the reservoir area." *from* https://www.sitecproject.com/sites/default/files/info-sheet-site-c-reservoir-feb-2018_0.pdf, published by BC Hydro.

[72] http://www.amnesty.ca/our-work/campaigns/site-c

Alaska Highway in 1942, and because the oil industry had already brought tens of thousands of newcomers. Power generation in other provinces is much more isolated from the lives of urban people. Yet hydro power development and the ensuing destruction of ecosystems are the focus of many other struggles in Canada involving treaty rights of Indigenous peoples. The politics of electrical power are such that, faced with rival statistics and contradictory claims and studies regarding future needs for power at predictable prices, politicians seem time after time to decide for development over environment and respect for the treaties. If their bets on prices and needs are wrong, however, it will mean that land and ecosystems are lost for nothing. The jury of the future will decide, even as many people will continue to lament and vigorously protest the loss of the river valley.

On other resource fronts, the collapse of the US housing industry in the world financial crisis of 2008 and decline in demand for lumber, compounded by ongoing difficulties with trade agreements for softwood lumber exports to the USA, and changes to the BC Forest Act that have allowed lumber to be processed outside the region where it is cut, all caused the forest industry in the North Peace to falter. Some say it has been devastated.[73] The Canfor plants in Fort Nelson, which made plywood and OSB (oriented strand board—key in home construction), shut down, and the railway was forced to reduce its schedule. A forest industry revitalization committee, along with the Fort Nelson First Nation, has been trying to find ways to rebuild the local industry, and in the Throne Speech on February 13, 2018, the BC government indicated at last that it would act to restore the proviso that timber harvested from Crown land be processed in the community.[74]

The oil industry, pulp and paper industry, and mining—all resource extraction activities—have brought prosperity and thousands of people to the North Peace region. Sustainability and culture are still issues, and the concerns of Indigenous people remain to be addressed. In some ways, the province has moved forward, in others not, given the Site C dam was approved without the consent of all the region's first peoples.

When John Callison first arrived in the Fort St. John area, Indigenous peoples were almost 100% of the area's population.

---

[73] Jonny Wakefield. "Fort Nelson struggles to rebuild 'devastated' forestry sector." Alaska Highway News, Dec. 5, 2016.
[74] http://bccfa.ca/horgan-wants-to-revitalize-the-forest-industrys-social-contract-with-british-columbians/

Currently, they represent about 11.7% (15.3% in the BC Peace Regional District overall).[75] Despite their smaller percentage of the population, and continual government attempts at assimilation and cultural suppression, they have persisted as nations and cultures. Today they take the lead in progressive politics, by proposing, financing, and co-managing projects that practise more ecologically sound extraction techniques, to increase the chance of protecting animals and terrain.

All in all, it is critical for the future of everyone to bring together Indigenous visions and ethics of stewardship of the land and its sacred gifts with the pioneer and settler visions of economic prosperity.

It is a work in progress to this day.

John Callison, Grand Haven hills above the Peace River, early 1990s. These lands will be flooded if the Site C Dam is built.

---

[75] "Aboriginal Populations Climb in BC and across Canada." *Alaska Highway News*, October 26, 2017. The article has links to 2016 Canadian Census data. http://www.alaskahighwaynews.ca/regional-news/aboriginal-populations-climb-in-b-c-and-across-canada-1.23076177

VIGNETTE: *"Just a minute!"*

This chapter on changes and the land wouldn't be complete without a few words about George Behn, headman of the Behn family, former Chief of the Fort Nelson First Nation and past Grand Chief of the Treaty 8 Tribal Association, and respected Elder, who heard his first words of English from Lynch Callison.

George was born December 18, 1924, in Old Fort Nelson. His parents having died when he was young, he lived with his grandmother till she became too old to look after him, at which point he went to live with Arthur and Lodema George at their store. He was adept and a fast learner; he'd worked a trapline inherited from his grandfather since he was ten. When Anne was in Old Fort Nelson working, he would have been 19 years old, and had already worked guiding the Americans surveying the Alaska Highway near the Kledo River, as did the Callisons. "Mr. and Mrs. George done a lot for me, you know. What little experience I got, you know, in the white man's world, I got good experience from them. Like schooling. I never went to school because there was no facility. But I worked with the girls that worked for them, you know, after hours. It all depends how tired they were. I used to study with them at night. Even after I was married, I used to go to the teacher and get some school books for a week. I used to study by the campfire, in the winter time. So, that's where I learned to read and write a bit."

George talks of other changes: the appearance of more horses in the area, for example, whereas prior to the highway, his people had relied more on packdogs and their own two feet. "I knew that country, born and raised. Like a squirrel, I guess."

In the same interview,[76] he talks of the first words he heard in English as a child: "In the spring time, scouts brought supplies down the Sikanni, to the Old Fort, and on down. There was four or five freighters got scouts lined up there along the shore. And my grandmother had a night line for fish. So me and my cousin, we went down there, and these people over here, and we got a couple of fish. We come up the little path onto the trail, and we said, well maybe somebody will come and take the fish away from us. Then here's this guy coming and talking away, and I don't know what he was saying, but I remember to this day, just like he said it this morning: *"Just a minute."* I remember that word well. But we didn't know what it meant. We just took off into the bush, hid our fish and went home. That guy was Lynch Callison. A well-known family, those guys. Good trappers, good hunters. I worked for them for many years. I had lots of experience from them, you know. Tough as a nail. Yeah. I remember one, I used to work for him, you know, and... We get up for breakfast at six o'clock, okay. If some guy is still staggering around [after a late card game, perhaps], he'll come in and just say "Hey, it's six o'clock. You're still sleeping. How do you expect to get a day's work in?"

---

[76]Quotes from *George Behn interview,* part of the Royal BC Museum's Living Landscape Series, conducted by Tourism Dawson Creek on June 27, 2004. Online.

On November 19, 1992, George, as Grand Chief of the Treaty 8 Tribal Association, gave testimony to the Royal Commission on Aboriginal Peoples[77] of the changes wrought by logging, clear-cutting in particular, on their traplines and ability to hunt, and spoke of water contamination and other damage to the land and warned of its effects on future generations.

George Behn was later the protagonist in a famed blockade in 2006 to prevent logging that would destroy his traplines. He had not been advised of the consultation with the Fort Nelson First Nation, and was only made aware of the permits when he received the order to remove his traps in the summer of 2006. His objections were disqualified then. He advised all in July 2006 that he intended to stop the logging. In early October, "Mr. Behn, who was 82 at the time, set up a folding chair on an access road leading into the license area.... He and members of his family spent the next three months peacefully maintaining the blockade, largely preventing work from continuing at the site. As the blockade dragged on, Moulton was left unable to sell timber, and its suppliers repossessed much of the company's logging equipment. The licenses later expired."[78] After years in court, the BC Supreme Court judge concluded in 2013 that BC had not meaningfully consulted with the Nation about the logging proposal, "particularly since the band was not equipped to properly assess such projects and their potential impact." The judge wrote in the findings for damages: "I cannot find that the province consulted with (Fort Nelson First Nation) in a manner sufficient to maintain the honour of the Crown." The Behns were absolved from liability, and BC was ordered to pay the logging company $1.75 million damages. On appeal by the BC government in February 2015, the damages judgement was quashed. In October 2015, the logging company asked the Supreme Court for leave to appeal that decision, but their application was dismissed.

Today, in February 2018, the Fort Nelson First Nation is working with the municipality to obtain a long-term community forest license for harvesting timber in the area, keeping resources and benefits in the communities.

To learn more about the Behns and the Fort Nelson First Nation and their territory today, watch *Fractured Land*, a prize-winning film by Damien Gillis and Fiona Rayher (Two Island Films, 2015).[79]

---

[77] *Royal Commission on Aboriginal Peoples - Transcriptions of Public Hearings and Round Table Discussions, 1992-1993.* Minister of Public Works and Government Services, and Privy Council Office: 2008, 166-180. The Commission was struck in 1991 to make recommendations on Crown relations with Indigenous peoples in Canada; their report was first issued in 1996. Many of the recommendations have still not been implemented.

[78] James Keller. "BC Government ordered to pay logging company 1.75M$ over aboriginal blockade." CTV News, December 30, 2013.

[79] The film is about one of George Behn's grandsons: environmental activist, orator, and lawyer Caleb Behn.

Children Grown Up
New generation, new dreams

While the oil industry was still in its infancy, Anne and John were raising their family in Dawson Creek and taking care of farm and motel, and also getting back to the trapline. The post-war boom that followed the construction of the highway was still in progress. It seemed big at the time, but was very modest compared with what was to come!

Wayne and Adley at 3 and 4 years old with Kledo the sled dog, 1949.

Anne and John's youngest son Darcey Brent was born in Dawson Creek in 1953, and went to school there until moving south to complete his high school where he could better pursue his interest in drama and dance. His brothers completed high school in Dawson Creek.

Adley, a powerful swimmer and diver as well as a horseman, went on to work in the oil exploration industry as a deep-sea diver at ocean-based drilling platforms around the world, from the East Asian seas around Singapore, to the Caribbean, Newfoundland, and England. Anne recalls he was renowned for his ability to dive and find and repair problems. He spent years away from Canada in his chosen career, later working as a supervisor of drilling operations. When divers from

151

Vancouver came to work on structural projects on the Peace River, Adley, back in Canada, was employed as a senior advisor. From the age of four, he's also been a talented musician and singer, and still sings and plays the guitar. Later, he returned to the Montney valley to raise horses and cattle, and raised his first family of two boys, Clinton and Dustin. Clinton now lives in Maple Ridge, BC and runs an insurance agency in the Lower Mainland, and Dustin is in Fort St. John and is a welder. Adley lives at Murdale once more today, along with his wife and daughter, continuing the family tradition of farming and ranching.

Wayne left the North Peace as well, to attend UBC in Vancouver, where he took Commerce. The third or fourth of the Callisons in his generation to graduate from university,[80] Wayne later qualified as a chartered accountant. After graduating, the lure of the North beckoned him back, and he joined a regional accounting practice in its Smithers, BC office. His children—three sons and a daughter—are now grown and most live in the Lower Mainland, pursuing a variety of careers, though one works with him in Smithers as an accountant. All four obtained degrees from UBC, their father's alma mater.

Darcey is also talented as a singer, musician, and dancer. After a Masters degree in dance and choreography at Simon Fraser University in Vancouver, Darcey plunged into Montreal's dance performance scene. In 1990, shifting his base to Toronto, he founded a contemporary dance company, Da Collision, for which he has choreographed many works that have been performed across Canada and in Mexico. As an associate professor in the acclaimed Dance program at York University, Darcey has been instrumental in the creation of Canada's first graduate programs in Dance Dramaturgy. As well as teaching dance, he is active in research and creation; his practice brings together choreography, postmodern dance methodologies, and new media and cultural studies. He is the first of his family to hold a doctorate in his field.

The Callison story has now moved further from histories of immigration and settlement, and has become by and large a story of life *off* the land—a story shared by most descendents of the first settlers in the Peace River Country.

With their circle of family complete, and the passing of their parents and many of their siblings, Anne and John Callison turned their attentions to the future: to grandchildren, and community service.

---

[80] Cousin Garry Callison QC studied law and worked as a lawyer in Fort St. John for +40 years.

Horses, Cattle, and Land
John in his later years

John Callison very much loved caring for the land that was his heritage at Murdale. He farmed until he was 85, though at times the fields were rented out to other farmers. Once retired, he travelled a lot with Anne, up the Alaska Highway, in BC and Alberta to visit family, and back to North Dakota and to Tempe, Arizona for family reunions. They travelled abroad, as well, visiting twelve different countries. John's love, though, was raising cattle and growing what was needed to sustain them in the Montney Valley. He planted fescue, hay, peavine, and other crops.

John also followed the call of his adopted Catholic faith. He joined the Knights of Columbus in December 1954, soon after moving his family to the city, in Dawson Creek, and was a staunch advocate for them all his life, participating regularly in Assembly meetings and at social functions with his wife Anne. His presence touched many lives. He was a fourth degree Knight of Columbus, a life member of the Elks, and a dedicated Catholic church association volunteer. He was a fan of country music, and loved teaching and playing with his grandchildren, hunting, farming, fishing, and trapping. He was always a quiet man, in a reserved and kind way. There was a generosity to his presence that was palpable to everyone, old and young.

In the early 1970s, with all his sons away in their own careers or in university, John's nephew Bill Moure spent two summers up at Fort St. John with John and Anne. One year, they both spent some weeks at Murdale, fixing up a cabin that had been skidded onto the land across the road from the original homestead, to live in it. Bill remembers John saying repeatedly that he wanted to work up the land again.

At one point that summer, John bought a expensive new big four-wheel drive tractor to replace his old one. No sooner, Bill remembers, did he get it delivered to the farm when it broke down. It soon became apparent that the tractor would have to go back to the dealer, and they waited so long for the part, that John just took up using his 1949-vintage two-cylinder Model-R John Deere (first Deere with a diesel motor) again until he could find a newer second-hand tractor, a Deere 5020. It was an infamous tale of trading old for new, and of the hazards of progress that sometimes send you backwards!

In those summers, Bill, barely a teenager and raised in Calgary, learned a lot about farming and machinery from John, Anne, and others, and about fishing, caring for land, hunting animals, and living the kind of life that John had been living when Anne first met him.[81] It might have been anachronistic—the urban world was then in the midst of the hippie era—but Bill learned resourcefulness that led him onward in life. He too grew up to be a farmer, a provider of moosemeat, a skilled fisherman, and capable of being autonomous in the bush.

Bill still remembers John's physical strength with admiration. John was always active, and never ate or drank to excess, so he was a wiry and muscular man. Bill recalls working with John. "Sometimes when his back was sore, he'd pull his shirt off and I'd rub Absorbine Jr on it.[82] Even when he was in his 60s," Bill said, "he looked like a bodybuilder." Anne once told young Bill proudly that John could do fifty push-ups. "What are you talking about?" said Bill, age 14. "I can do fifty push-ups!" Bill hit the ground and started counting them off, pushing up with his hands placed under his shoulders. "Oh," said John, "so that's what you call a push-up." Bill stopped. "And what do you call a push-up?" John demonstrated from a standing position, his hands at his hips not his shoulders. Bill tried it and, he recalls, "I might have managed *two*!"

When John and Bill were summering at Murdale that year, Anne would drive up regularly to pay them a visit. Sometimes she'd stay a day or so, sometimes not. When she was there, John and Bill would stick closer to the cabin and keep Anne company.

"When she was there," Bill said, "we'd sit and have tea in the afternoons. And you know how Anne loves her tea." One time she was praising how the tea had reenergized her, saying: "Oh my that tea was good! I bet I could run a race." She turned to Bill: "I bet I could beat you in a race!" So out the door they went, right to the road, agreeing to

---

[81] As a youngster, Bill had already tried to emulate his Uncle John—by winter camping in the woods, fishing, and even trapping in the Elbow River in Calgary. He managed to catch a few muskrat, which he skinned and sold to Simpson and Lea, the last fur buyer in the city. So he did get a taste of that bygone era!

[82] Sandy, granddaughter of Pat Callison (daughter of Joan), calls Absorbine Jr. "the Callison Cure-all," familiar to the whole family. "My mother swears by it and my grandfather used it liberally for almost any cut, blemish, ache, or ailment. When I was young, Uncle John even used it on his head as a tonic to help his hair grow!"

race a half a mile. Anne looked Bill up and down, and decided to change the rules, saying: "Oh but you have to run backwards!" Backwards! No problem: Anne was so full of tea that Bill quickly passed her, then ran backwards right in front of her, grinning. "She started laughing, watching me looking at her. Soon she was laughing so hard she could hardly walk, and had to stop running. We never made it half a mile, only 50 yards. We both staggered back to the cabin in gales of laughter."

Anne made the footrace famous by retelling the story to all and sundry. She still does it today. "Say, did you hear about the footrace?"

In the 1980s, John's arthritis reached a point where he needed hip replacements, and he was sent to Vancouver to have them done, one then the other. Anne was very worried about the outcome, as hip replacements were far less common then, but John recovered well. Though he was told by doctors that he would never get on a horse again, Anne once claimed he did manage to get back up on a horse. "Once John decided to do something," Anne said, "he'd dedicate himself to the task till it was done."

Anne and John in retirement on their front porch in Fort St. John (9616 103 Ave).

VIGNETTE: Fishing with John Callison, by Bill Moure

When I lived up with them for two summers, John had a 28' river boat mostly used on the Peace River and Charlie Lake, and a Ford crew cab truck with a 8' box and a canopy over it. I'd never seen a crew cab before. He pulled the boat on a trailer behind, so the whole rig was over 50' long. When we went fishing, we camped in tents.

We made one trip out to Carp Lake. A road had been opened there for logging, the first road to reach the lake, and the public could use it at night, from midnight to 6 a.m., when logging trucks were not running. I remember it as a bad road and it took most of the time you were allowed on it to get to the water, so you had to line up with the others and be ready to start right at midnight. The road just went right to the lake with no place to pull off or park. John chopped down trees so that we could get the truck and trailer off the road, where it was safe to leave them. At Carp Lake, we hauled everything to an island in the lake with the boat. Probably camped 5 or 10 miles from where the road met the lake. The lakeshore was very wooded, impossible to find an open place to camp. The islands, however, were sandy and fairly open.

Another two families came with their vehicles and boats. I think we were there about a week; the others did not stay the same length of time. I remember John packing fish in moss in beer-bottle boxes for another family to take out with them when they left so that we could keep fishing and not exceed our limits. To keep the fish from spoiling, Anne was canning them on the Coleman stove, in jars. The ones we caught in the last couple of days were brought out fresh and then frozen when we got home. They were all rainbow trout.

There were a bunch of teens a little older than me. One day we tried water skiing behind their family's river boat, which had a bigger motor than John's. The water was very cold. I still have pictures of John and myself with fish at our camp.

A few years later, I visited Anne and John and asked them if they had been back to Carp Lake. They said no, it was fished out.

Only recently have people realized just how quickly fish stocks can be depleted. Other than stocked fish in the Elbow River, I was never able to catch fish in Alberta's mountain streams. Now that virtually all those streams are "catch and release," it is easy to catch fish there again. Turns out, when fishing, you have two choices. You can catch fish and let them go or you can not catch fish. I prefer the former.[83]

---

[83] email from Bill Moure, 2 December 2017.

Heading to shore from camping in Carp Lake, 1973.

Campsite on island at Carp Lake, 1973. John, Bill, a day's catch of trout, and
Anne's shadow (the photographer!)

Hills of the Montney Valley from the homestead at Murdale, August 2017.

John Deere 5020 from 1972, survivor of the 4WD tractor fiasco, at rest in 2017.

Organizing for Community
Anne in her later years

VIGNETTE: One Very Busy Woman

In Anne Callison's files, on the back of the page with her carrot cake recipe, there is a scribbled fall banquet schedule for the CWL 1970 and 1971 seasons leading up to Christmas. You can see how busy Anne was!

"1970:
    October 17: LAA (ours)
    November 14: P. Smith
    Nov. 20: Oilmens evening (ours)
    Nov. 28: NW Radio A.
    Dec. 11: Westcoast
    Dec 12: School Maintenance
    Dec 19: Pacific Pet (ours)
1971:
    Dec. 4
    Dec 11
    Dec 18"

Even when there was no plan, Anne was scheming! Maybe that's why, when Anne's asked what they did in the old days for entertainment, her famous answer is: *Oh, we had work to entertain us!* (Of course, as we know... she also had footraces!)

With the three boys grown and off on their own, Anne threw her energies into the Dawson Creek and then Fort St. John CWL. To round out her work life, which started in the late 1930s working at Bear Lake, with stints home-nursing the sick (John's mother, her own mother and Dad, Winnie Callison, Mollie Callison, Mrs. Rosalie Clay, Jean Craig, Delores Schubert) and working as a nurse's aide at the Providence Hospital in High Prairie, Alberta, she also had a long career as a hospital volunteer for the Auxiliary at the Providence Hospital in Fort St. John.

Anne is a dedicated volunteer.[59] She served as President of the Catholic Women's League in Fort St. John for her parish from 1985-1987, and has been an active member of that organization for over sixty

---

[59] Sandy Baker. "Peace Country Pioneer and Volunteer, Anne Callison." *The Flipside,* May 2012.

years; as well she is a life member of the Royal Purple, the Fort St. John North Peace Museum Society, and the Peace Lutheran Care Centre Foundation. She volunteered variously at Resurrection Parish for forty years, working on initiatives for prayer and peace in South Africa, raising money for Christmas dinners and gifts for the needy, kids' summer camps, the school and public library, Women's Transition House, the Extended Care Unit at the hospital, refugees, etc. She took seminars offered on everything from leadership training to learning to pray, co-organized many regional conferences, and attended talks by visiting speakers on socially critical subjects such as hunger and family violence. As a member of the Fort St. John's Hospital Auxiliary, she volunteered every Monday in the Hospital Gift Shop for many years too, and was a familiar and consoling figure to those who came to visit the sick.

Anne enjoyed playing a lead organizing role in several of the CWL's annual International Parish Banquets, which included a procession, holiday wreath, representatives from the city of Fort St. John, the Knights of Columbus, the RCMP, the Parish Pastor, as well as a Pipe Band, guitar player, and food and evening entertainment from as many countries of origin as possible: French, Slovak, German, Swiss, Polish, English, Native Canadian, Canadian, Dutch, Ukraine, Italy, South Africa, Ireland, and the Philippines! At the banquet on December 2, 1978, for example, they started by singing "It's A Small World After All." The meal was served after the procession, which involved volunteers carrying in the food that represented their nation for placement at the buffet table, before O Canada was sung and grace said.

At such annual suppers, there was entertainment, of course: a pipe band, an Irish soloist singing the Connemara Cradle Song and Willie McBride, a Philippine Christmas song, an Irish dance group, Polish group singing a Polish and a Ukrainian Christmas carol, a Mexican hat dance, a solo Christmas carol in German, and a French-Canadian contribution. People of the Peace shared their pride in their origins and in the contribution each group made to the settler community.

Anne Callison had learned well from her time working with Mrs. Lodema George at the trading post in Fort Nelson; she knew how to keep a team of women organized, how to make sure there would be enough food, and even that the kitchen would be cleaned up at the end and leftovers sent home in peoples' cars. Her lists of things to do always included everything from the cake recipe to the number of garbage bags and boxes needed to clean up.

Anne seated bottom left, with CWL colleagues at a buffet table, 1980s.

Anne also cherished records of her family history. She has kept all the mass cards and the memorial book for her mother, Nelly Grendys, who died Nov 22, 1963. The package accompanies her still.

Throughout the 1970s, Anne regularly returned to the Grande Prairie area of her first Canadian home on Saskatoon Mountain, to visit her father Tom in the Pioneer Home in Hythe, Alberta. Tom, beloved father, grandfather, and great-grandfather died at the age of 100 on Christmas Day, 1977.

Anne remembers one alarming travel incident from her road trips, and her telling of it is characteristic of Anne's spunky good humour. "I went to visit my Dad at the Pioneer Home in Hythe in winter. It was icy driving down, and near Hythe, I rolled my car; it ended up with its wheels facing the sky. We didn't use seatbelts in those days, and I was thrown from front seat to back. When the car came to a stop, I grabbed my purse and got out, hitched a ride and made it to Hythe and went to the doctor." She was so in shock when she arrived (though appearing entirely competent) that she asked the doctor: "Am I sick? Am I dead?" On the third day after the accident, she went out curling, a favourite winter sport. "I opened my purse," she says, "and there was broken glass in it! Who knows how the windshield got in there! But I didn't have a scar, scratch, or bruise. I was just fine."

For the British Columbia Winter Games held in Fort St. John in 1984, Anne Callison was called upon to organize the catering of meals with her CWL team. It was probably the largest job she'd taken on. Afterward, she received congratulations and thanks from the BC premier, in a letter she still treasures.

Whenever big civic groups came through town, and needed banquets, she'd work with others to organize meals, clean-up, and then thank her volunteers at the end of it all by throwing them a wine and cheese party. She was appreciative, worked tirelessly herself, and was considerate of others, though very persuasive. If Anne Callison thought you should take on a chore or a job, you thought twice before you said no! So everyone pitched in and worked with her, and she made it seem fun. At one large event they were catering, the local Vocational School came, for a class project on nutrition, to check out and analyze the quality of her menus. Their conclusion was unanimous: the menus reflected a simple but balanced diet.

For Anne, the CWL and other organizations were places of fellowship, helping, and belonging. She always came with a word of encouragement, a joke, or a story to keep up morale. She had a stock of quotes she'd found, and shared them for inspiration. In her words, her goal has always been to "bring love, hope and peace into individual lives, and lend a helping hand where most needed." In her archive papers, she writes: "Life is not a path for us alone; we must learn to work with others." She records five simple rules for happiness, which sum up a philosophy that this book shares with all her readers today:

1. Free your heart from hatred.
2. Free your mind from worries.
3. Live simply.
4. Give more.
5. Expect less.

Callison Homecoming 1987 at Fort St. John,
and 50th Wedding Anniversary 1994

Reunions and reunions! They bring together far-flung family and relations, and help maintain memory across generations. Anne and John Callison enthusiastically attended several, in North Dakota—of Callisons and Lynches, and in Tempe, Arizona in February 1990, of Callisons— and held their own festivities as well.

From July 3-5, 1987 at Fort St. John and Murdale, John and Anne held a huge homecoming reunion. Anne felt that the Callison era was slowly fading; not many of the original Fred Callison family were left, and they were largely scattered. In Anne's words: "Progress started. As time went on, each member of the family left the area to fuel their own dreams. John, for the love of land and animals, stayed on." Anne wanted the next generation to have the chance to meet and be aware of their shared heritage.

"The Reunion was truly a happy time, with horseshoes, volleyball, a crib tournament, horseback riding and hiking, and bonfires at night with singing and music, all offered freely to everyone, as we'd done all our lives. It was truly a small piece of history and a time of peace."

Anne and John, 1994.

VIGNETTE Anne Callison's philosophy

Anne spoke to the assembled generations of Callisons at the 1987 family reunion. She had gathered quotes from many sources that she had made her own over the years. She offered them on many public occasions in different combinations, and they are worth citing here, copied from her notes.

With God as our guide
success is a journey,
not a destination.
Happiness is to be found along the way
not at the end of the road.
For then the journey is over
and it is too late.
Today, this hour, this minute
it's time for each of us to sense the fact that
life is good with all its trials and tribulations
and perhaps is more interesting
because of them.
Life is uncharted territory.
It reveals its story one moment at a time.
What you give away in life
is what you keep.

John and Anne celebrated their 50th wedding anniversary on July 10, 1994 with a big party at the famed Grand Haven Dance Hall—a hexagonal log building decorated with moose antlers—just south of Fort St. John. It was attended by 150 friends and relatives from as far away as Toronto, Surrey, Calgary and Fort Nelson. My mother Mary attended; there was no way she'd be anywhere else but by her sister's side!

By then, says Anne, just three others of Fred and Dora Callison's family were left: Norma, Daisy, and Dennis. John and Anne were proud of the letters of congratulations they received from the City of Fort St. John, MP Jay Hill, MLA Richard Neufeld, and blessings from Pope John Paul II. On July 12, the Catholic Women's League held another celebration and mass for the couple at the Peace Lutheran Care Home.

John and Anne Callison lived lives that, when taken together, span pretty much all of the 20th century and go a good distance into the 21st, from John's birth in 1909 to the completion of this book in 2018. Their lives have been ones of hard work, and of an ethics of service to their communities and family. At the time of their 50th wedding anniversary, they had six grandchildren: Dustin and Clinton (sons of Adley) in Fort St. John, and Justin, Dorian, Aiden, and Haleigh in Smithers BC (sons and daughter of Wayne). More recently, Anne has a seventh grandchild, the spirited Isobel, and several great grandchildren.

There were other family occasions that Anne remembers, among them the annual or biannual Lynch family reunions in Halliday, North Dakota, where the Fred Callison and Dora Lynch, newly married, first homesteaded, living in a sod house that was destroyed by a tornado a few weeks after they emigrated to Canada.

The Lynch reunions were held regularly in the 1980s and 1990s. Anne Callison took the bus to attend the fourth reunion in July 1996 in Halliday (just months after John died in May of that year), and brought back a notebook full of entries and comments from those relatives who attended, and with records of the family cattle brands. The Lynch-Callison family was vast and had spread far and wide, and their descendants were employed in a vast array of fields and professions, all dutifully recorded: construction worker, carpenter, rancher, sheriff, exercise physiologist, artist (many!), oil plant worker, welder, counsellor, farrier, doctor, receptionist, hairdresser, civil servant, nurse, social worker, engineer, conservation officer, physical therapist, stone mason, mariner, etc. The reunions bustled: at one lunch, they grilled 80 pounds of lemon-pepper chicken! Every morning in Halliday, Anne got up and walked 2 miles at 6 a.m. with her hostess.

In the midst of the hubbub, on the day of her departure in 1996 on July 10, Anne made a special note: "John's and my 52nd wedding anniversary today. Kathryn and I walked 2½ miles, had breakfast. Kathryn drove me to Dickinson where I took her to lunch, before parting at 1:55 p.m. on the bus. Had a great visit with every one. Glad I made it to the reunion."

VIGNETTE: Recognizing Kindness

Recognizing and thanking others is something Anne Callison has done all her life. She's been modest about her own accomplishments, and today there is a quiet dignity to her presence. In the February 18, 2016 edition of the local paper, the Alaska Highway News, there appears this small article, with no further comment, from Anne at the age of 94, who was then still living on her own in an apartment for seniors. It's very typical of Anne!

An act of kindness, a heart of gold
Alaska Highway News
FEBRUARY 18, 2016 07:38 AM
To the lady who so kindly paid for my groceries at the Wholesale Club on Feb.11, I would like to thank you from the bottom of my heart. I didn't get your name, but you have a heart of gold.
Anne Callison, Heritage Manor, Fort St. John

Anne and John Callison in Tempe, AZ, February 1990.

The Callison Story

A Ballad by Anne Callison

The Callisons loved ballads as forms of poetry, song, and historical record. Different members of the family often took to long ballad-like poems to express, retain, and communicate family history. The impulse was a natural one, for there is a long tradition of poetry's presence when history comes into play. Poems used to be published in newspapers to commemorate events, and many settler families took up that tradition, composing rhymed narrative poems for happenings of great importance. Often there was a bit of humour injected just from the attempts at forced rhyme. Some of these poems are worth keeping, as they hold a lot of history in just a few words. This poem appears often in different typescripts and copies in Anne Callison's papers, and was surely recited at the Callison Family Homecoming at Fort S. John in 1987. It takes its inspiration from the classic Robert Service poem of the North, "The Cremation of Sam McGee," which would have been known and appreciated by all.

It is true strange things were done
by the Callison Sons
As they helped open up this land.   *myth of the pioneer, that the land was empty*
But strange as it seems
There were many dreams
That came true for this noble band.

There was Fred and Henry who came first
To satisfy their unquenchable thirst
For adventure, in this land of snow.   *winters were indeed cold*
They trapped the furs
And rode with spurs   *horses, furs, dog-teams all featured strongly*
And dogteam they did go.   *in daily life at the time*

Fred took Dora to be his bride,
And together they toiled side by side.   *respect for women's work is shown;*
they raised five sons and daughters four.   *toil is hard and relentless work*
Hardships many they had to bear
But for Dora and Fred complaints are rare,   *accepting hardship without complaint*
And the family grew and prospered more.

The eldest was Lynch, the life of the party
He had many jobs until he was past forty.
Then came John a trapper at heart   *trapping was vital to John's identity; it was a*
But he and wife Anne had a motel   *way of being a breadwinner*
The family farm, the Homestead as well,
Each one playing a successful part.

Pat came next with his writing flair   *the creation of books was highly valued*
And his love for travel, be it land or air.
His "Pack Dogs to Helicopters" is quite renowned.
It tells of his life and his escapades
These adventures time will never fade.
His love of family is fond and sound.

Daughter Norma, married a Baillie
Who took care of her almost daily,
And they had a brood of seven.
And Lash (Elijah) by name   *Elisha, born Aug 30, 1914, at Pouce Coupe*
Was a rancher of quite some fame   *married Winnie Parker in 1936*
The Northland became his Heaven.

Doris married a Bud (not a rose)   *William (Bud) Simpson*
But working together they never froze
While they managed the Rancheria Motel.   *motel, service station, café near Watson Lake*
Along with a family of five,
All managed to survive
Now they are retired with tales to tell.

Dennis and Daisy the Callison twins,
Made many a problem for kith and kin.
Dennis an outfitter and hunting guide,   *also a hotelier... with wife Marj, ran Toad*
Daisy an artist of some design   *River Lodge at Mile 422 of Alaska Highway*
She paints pictures, a very fine line
Their talents neither can hide.

The youngest is Mollie, the last in the line.
This young lady married and did quite fine.
But then all were successful in their way of life,
Either trapping, or ranching or Motel enterprise.
All were a credit, which is no great surprise,
For the hardships endure, mid the woes and strife.   *again, hints at the difficult times*

Henry, the younger brother of Fred
Left his love of trapping for the Homestead.
His wife and three daughters made up his life
Delores and Jean and Gay — all girls

Left Henry no time to sit or curl
For he was busy with plough and scythe.

"History repeats itself" is a well-known fact
Five more Callisons may take the track
The grandsons of John and Anne.
This is a wish that these five boys   *written before Haleigh Callison was born...*
Carry the torch that courage employs
Of those stalwart sons of the Callison Clan.   *plus Haleigh, renowned hockey star!*

We give thanks to God that these pioneers
Had the foresight to immigrate here.
Their origin dates from across the sea.
Men of the Cloth, men of law and order,
Coming here from across the border,
Making this land, by love and toil, for all to see.

VIGNETTE from a speech at John and Anne's 50th wedding anniversary

John was always a very serious, honest, and respected individual. When trapping. he taught other trappers better ways of doing things, such as skinning, etc. To show how honest John is, I'll tell you a little story. One time on the highway a policeman put on his siren and pulled John over. John immediately grabbed his seatbelt and strapped it on. The policeman approached John's car and asked: "Did you have your seatbelt on?" John looked at him and answered: "No, I didn't."

John, 1936, second from right, with a bear; John in 1994.

VIGNETTE: Gentleman John

...(...) John Callison's life spanned a century: from travelling on the original steam trains to witnessing men land on the moon. He was an original Peace River pioneer, a self-made man building his life from the land by hard work and determination. By necessity, he learned to hunt, trap, and farm at an early age, and then was able to use these skills to build a successful life for himself and his family. Farming his land in Montney was always an important part of John's life. He continued to plough and work this homestead until he was 85, and we feel sure that if he had his way, he would still be ploughing it. When able, he would willingly help out others; people nicknamed him Gentleman John and Honest John, names that reflected the values he lived by and the manner in which he treated people. If a man can be measured by the respect of his family, friends, and acquaintances, John Callison was a fine man who met every measure, a man we are all proud to have known. He passed away on May 12, 1996, and his funeral was held at the Church of the Resurrection in Fort St. John on May 16.

The Alaska Highway News, September 20, 1996

A Land of Change
best memories and hopes for the future

Famed scientist and conservationist David Suzuki talks about how the lands of the North Peace—on which the Callisons and their children lived and flourished—have been subject to such extensive usage changes that the future will be much different than the past, and the past will be harder to evoke. That's one reason why Anne Callison felt it was crucial to tell her story and that of her family: a story told from a woman's perspective, a story of what happened in the 20th century, of what is left unresolved, of what was accomplished.

Despite the tremendous changes over the course of the past century—from the world of the fur trade and of bush self-sufficiency experienced by only a few white people (and fewer other newcomers) in lands that for millennia were territory that belonged to the Dane-ẕaa, the Tse'kene, and the Cree, to a populated land under pressure from resource extraction and developments largely created to benefit those in cities far away—there are still hope and dreams.

The story of the future will be one that takes care of these lands, I hope, and considers the vitality of *all* the populations, animal and human, Indigenous and newcomer, caribou, moose, and beaver. It will be a story that values the air and water quality, the forests. It will remember the past, as well—the wars of Europe, the brutal effects of colonization—and will steer a course that brings fewer harms.

You who read these words will be among those who will be empowered to decide how the future is lived.

"What you give away in life is what you keep" is a Kurdish proverb, and a favourite of Anne's. Consumption and accumulation of wealth are not the true riches: what you keep, the real riches, come from generosity, from giving to others.

In the video interview often quoted here, Anne was asked what advice she would have for future generations. She replied without hesitation: "We need more volunteers." It is a way of bringing a lot of pleasure to peoples' lives, she explains, both to the volunteers' lives and to the lives of those who are helped. "You can't just be after the almighty dollar; you have to do something for nothing to be truly happy."

Anne Callison has been generous with her life and her story, and has allowed me—nourished by the moosemeat of childhood and my own small part in this family—to speak of her life and of that of my Uncle John against the backdrop of change and history. With Anne Callison, I too hold that the best hope for the future is for a world in which Isobel, her granddaughter, along with all the grandchildren and upcoming generations of all the inhabitants of the Peace River Country and beyond, can live fruitfully and happily. May this book of Anne's help you.

Here's to the future!

Anne Callison, late 1930s at Saskatoon Mountain and in a Fort St. John restaurant with Isobel, December 15, 2017 when Anne turned 96 and Isobel was 6.

Reading Anne Callison's Archives
an epilogue

To help Anne Callison fulfill her dream of memory, and create the book of her life and times, I have had to bury myself in two briefcases of papers that are her irreplaceable possessions of value. She's carried them everywhere all her life, and thank goodness, as after her stroke, they became part of her voice. They are Anne's own archives, and I am privileged to work in them.

I just have to write a small epilogue to describe their delights, because in the other chapters I've only mined their words, transposing them, augmenting those words with much research and many more words of my own. But Anne's papers hold small delights in the *material* sense; in them, I discover small paper sculptures that model the way Anne's mind works. She treasures so much that is held in writing, and has kept many writings that may seem cryptic or irrelevant at first glance, but which hold her memory, and in which memory overlaps and one memory cradles another memory that may be quite unlike it. In Anne's archives these memories touch each other, infinitely and forever.

Or perhaps not forever, which is why I add these words. For when the time comes for Anne to leave us, these archives may vanish into some greater archive (the Fort St. John North Peace Museum, perhaps) and be moved and reclassified, and some parts discarded. The materiality of the "sculpture" will be altered, and in some ways "un-Anned".

At the beginning of this book, I already spoke of one material archival gem: the photocopy of the Callison family Bible that held the marriage record of John's parents. On its reverse side of that photocopy, in Anne's hand, I found the scores from a game of cribbage! A game that livened many northern trapline nights (though this one I think was played with one of her sons one evening in the family living room or kitchen at the Callison Motel) is merged with the history of how her husband came to be, where he came from, and who his parents were.

I'd like to show you one more of those overlapping memory-archives of Anne Callison's. It is an envelope, the size of a small greeting card. Since it was postmarked on December 17, 1997 and comes from a company, it probably held a Christmas card, mailed to Anne, as a customer during the previous year. It comes from Northland Plumbing & Heating at 9315 – 100th Avenue, Fort St. John. A quick check of the phone book shows that today (in February 2018) the company still exists, a few doors down, at 9211 – 100th Avenue. It doesn't look like much in Google Street View, but there is a small older building there, and vehicles parked nearby. A modest company.

Anne's address on the envelope is 9616 – 103 Avenue, 11 minutes' walk from the plumbers. It looks on Google Street View like a large ranch-style home on a street of similar homes.

Inside the envelope, there is no card. There is a cutting from the Fort Nelson News, Wednesday February 19, 1997, so not long after that Christmas card was mailed, really. It is from page 12, I think, by the way the edges are cut, as it says page 11 on the little dateline snippet which, though not attached, must be related. The article is from the other side, which would be page 12, entitled "Herbal remedies take root, flourish," and is by Nanci Hellmich. There's a Nanci Hellmich who was a personal finance and lifestyle journalist for US Today from 1983 to 2015; she's a freelance health and lifestyle journalist today. There is no Nanci Hellmich in Fort Nelson. So it is a syndicated article. Perhaps Nanci Hellmich wasn't even paid for it, as by 1997 freelance wages were going down, and journalists were not paid for every reprint.

The article is about echinacea (colds and flu), garlic (cholesterol), St. John's wort (depression), ginseng (stress), and ginkgo biloba (age-related mental decline), but also says there's not enough science to back up the claims, and no government control to guarantee supplements contain what they say. Well, that's no different today! Anne does have an interest in health and natural remedies, remember: she tried to help John's arthritis with citrus, and when her sister was ill with cancer in 2005-7, she went down to Calgary to bring her rhubarb juice.

On the other side is part of a huge advertisement for Priceline.com, urging people to save money by using their site to buy their travel tickets. Name your price! it says. Hmmm. New cities are added every week! San Francisco, Seattle, St. Louis, Tampa/St. Pete and Washington DC are the cities visible in this part of the ad. All in the USA. Well, it's winter, February, people want to go south! And people in Fort St. John go to the USA, I guess.

But though Anne was interested in travel, in this case she was interested in health and herbs.

There's something else in the envelope. A folded paper. Stapled. More than one folded paper then. It's a letter from the JB Oliver Funeral home in Grande Prairie, AB addressed to Anne at Box 91, Dawson Creek, BC, dated November 27, 1963. Five days after her mother Anastasia (Nelly) died. It says it contains the title to her father's grave plot and receipt for payment to the City of Grande Prairie, operator of the cemetery. But the title and receipt attached with a staple are for Anastasia Grendys, her mother, not her father. Interestingly, the letter is addressed to Mrs. Anne Callison. In 1963, that would have been a bold way to insist on your name, if you were a woman, as technically, a married woman would be known as Mrs. John Callison. A widow would be known as Mrs. Anne Callison. Anne clearly was ready to assert her own first name, and John was ready to support her doing so. Not all husbands were willing to risk being thought of as dead! It took someone who treated his wife as a real partner, and felt it just that she *should* be called by *her* name, be called Anne instead of Mrs. John!

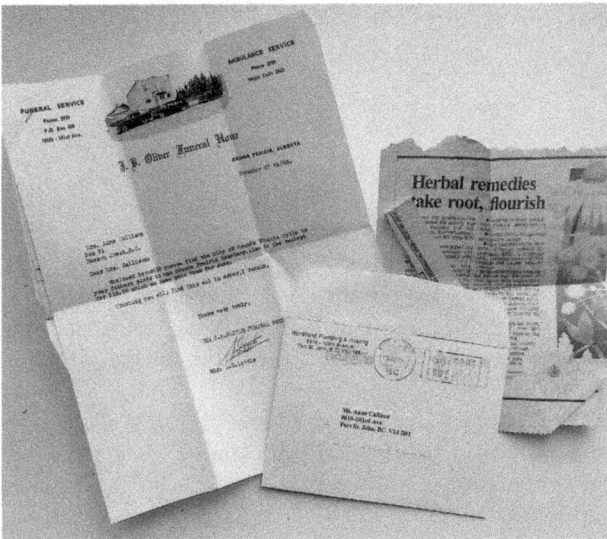

All her life, Anne has carried this folded reminder of her mother with her, and of her name. It holds a memory of where her mother is buried (for the plot number is there), and along with this memory—beside and touching it—is a thought on natural herbs and health, but also about honesty and safety, and truthfulness. As well, there is a memory of Christmas, an aching memory for it would have been Anne's first without her husband John (he died in May 1996), and an indication that no matter how many years go by, water flows where it will (so we need plumbers) and our mothers are always part of us, as is what we have learned from them about the natural world and about care.

All this resonates very powerfully in the materiality of this one item drawn from Anne Callison's archive. In turn, this envelope of papers presses against the other items held in the archive, resonating with rich

175

meanings that are Anne's thinking at work, holding what Anne treasures: mother, health, name, and the Peace River District—Fort Nelson, Fort St. John, Dawson Creek, and Grande Prairie.

VIGNETTE: Education and the Grendys Legacy

Mountain Trail School, in a photo taken by Anne's sister Mary in 1994: fallen in but still a mighty presence. Saskatoon Mountain, where Anne grew up after emigrating with her family from present-day Ukraine, is the hill in the background.

Education was key in both Anne's and Mary's lives; whereas Anne's was mostly informal, Mary did achieve high school graduation and studies as a registered nurse. Mary (my mother) always kept a photo of her first school at the junctions of Range Road 92 and Township Road 720, north of Huallen, Alberta.

Both Grendys sisters had a love and respect for the word and for the knowledge that words provide. This book is proof of Anne's love. Mary's children (Erín, Ken, and Bill) keep sharing our mother's dedication to education, to reading, and to libraries as essential for free thought by adopting a library through *CODE Canada*—currently one at King's School in Sierra Leone. If you wish to know more about the important work CODE Canada does to promote literacy in Canada and abroad, please visit www.code.ngo.

Acknowledgements and Bibliography

Big thanks to cousins Adley Callison, Wayne Callison, and brother Bill Moure for their collaboration and feedback. Extraordinary thanks to cousin Sandy Baker for her enthusiasm and support, and her research and editing/writing skills; this book is much better for her help. Thanks also to Anne Callison, Julia Havdale, Joan Rodschat, Shannon Callison, Mary Lister, Ken Moure, Shona Noble-Jones, Brent Grendys, Oksana Dudko, Taras Dudko, Sally Behn, and to my test readers, the writer/translators Robert Majzels and Lou Nelson.

Books and Articles

"Aboriginal Populations Climb in BC and across Canada." *Alaska Highway News*, Oct 26, 2017. The article has links to 2016 Canadian Census data. http://www.alaskahighwaynews.ca/regional-news/aboriginal-populations-climb-in-b-c-and-across-canada-1.23076177

Canadian Royal Commission on Aboriginal Peoples. *People to people, nation to nation: Highlights from the report of the Royal Commission on Aboriginal Peoples.* Ottawa: Supply and Services Canada, 1996.

Lake Saskatoon Reflections: A Local History of the Lake Saskatoon District, Sexsmith AB: Lake Saskatoon History Book Committee, 1980.

Multiple Authors. *Aboriginal Land and Resource Use Summary: Blueberry River First Nations*, from Site C Clean Energy Project, Volume 5 Appendix A03 Part 3, Final Report. BC Hydro, Vancouver, B.C. Prepared by Traditions Consulting, Victoria, B.C. January 2013.

Jan Anderson. "Callison Still Guiding the Way," *Interior News*, Smithers, BC. Reprinted in http://tahltan.ca/wp-content/uploads/2014/05/Tahltan-Band-May-2014.pdf May, 2014, 8.

Sandy Baker. "Peace Country Pioneer and Volunteer, Anne Callison." *The Flipside*. Dawson Creek, BC, May 2012.

Barry Broadfoot. *Six War Years 1939-1945*, Toronto: U Toronto Press, 1970.

Hugh Brody. *Maps & Dreams*. NY: Pantheon, 1982.

Daisy Callison. *Mountain Trails: A Prospecting Expedition from the Diary of a 16-year-old Girl, 1935*. Castlegar, BC: Havdale, 2004.

Pat Callison. *Pack Dogs to Helicopters: Pat Callison's Story*. Vancouver: Evergreen Press, 1983, 2nd edition 1984. By Athol Retallaek with Pat Callison.

Lily Gontard. *Beyond Mile Zero: The Vanishing Alaska Highway Lodge Community*. Madeira Park, BC: Harbour Publishing, 2017.

Theodore A. Huntley. *Construction of the Alaska Highway*. Seattle WA: National Archives, September 1943. http://www.themilepost.com/articles/construction-of-the-alaska-highway-first-year-1942-condensation-of-report-by-theodore-a-huntley-senior-administrative-officer-washington-september-1945/

Brenda Marie Ireland. *"Working a Great Hardship on Us": First Nations People, the State, and Fur Conservation in British Columbia before 1935*. Thesis. 1995. https://open.library.ubc.ca/cIRcle/collections/831/items/1.0086730 (an excellent resource on Indigenous experience).

Jack Jamieson. "Klondike." Profile of Pat Callison from *Western Wings*, May 1964. http://www.royalaviationmuseum.com/8834/article-klondike/

Eric Jensen. *Forever and a Day: The World War II Odyssey of an American Family*. Denver, CO: Outskirts Press, 2009.

Peter Lee and Matt Hanneman, for the David Suzuki Foundation and West Moberly First Nation. *Atlas of land cover, industrial land uses and industrial-caused land changes in the Peace Region of British Columbia* ISBN: 978-0-9780976-4-6. Edmonton: Global Forest Watch Canada, 2012.

Erín Moure. "Tuteshni." *Unbound: Ukrainian Canadians Writing Home*. ed. Lisa Grekul and Lindy Ledohowski. Toronto: U Toronto Press, 2016 (about returning to Velyki Hlibovychi with her mother's ashes).

Pioneer History Society of Hythe and Area. *Pioneer round-up: a history of Albright, Demmitt, Goodfare, Hythe, Lymburn, Valhalla*. Altona, MB: One Memory Lane, 1972.

Robin and Jillian Ridington with Elders of the Dane-ẕaa First Nations. *Where Happiness Dwells: A History of the Dane-ẕaa First Nations*. Vancouver: UBC Press, 2013.

Melanie Robinson. "Callison Family a part of history in the Northeast," *Northeast News*, Fort St. John, May 2, 2007, 28.

Rolla History Book Committee. *Rolla Remembers: 1912-1952*. Rolla AB, 1991.

Royal BC Museum. North to Alaska! A Personal Perspective of Building the Alaska Highway," Tourism Dawson Creek, 2005, part of the Living Landscapes series. Online.

Chester Russell. *Tales of a Catskinner*. Autumn Images, Fort Nelson BC: 2003.

E.C. Stacey. *Beaverlodge to the Rockies*. Beaverlodge, AB: Beaverlodge and District Historical Association, 1974.

Allison Tubman. *The McDonalds: Lives and Legends of a Kaska Dene Family*. Self-published, 2014. http://www.themcdonaldsbook.com/contact.html

Maj. Shawn M. Umbrell. *First on the Line: The 35th Engineer Battalion in World War Two and the Evolution of a High-Performance Combat Unit*. Master's thesis, U of Toledo, 1998, 52-53, online.

Cora Ventress with Marguerite Davies and Edith Kyllo. *The Peacemakers of North Peace*. Fort St. John: Davies Ventress and Kyllo, 1973.

John Virtue. *The Black Soldiers Who Built The Alaska Highway: 1942-43.* Jefferson, NC: McFarland & Co, 2013.

Gerri F. Young. *The Fort Nelson Story: the story of how a town grew out of the wilderness.* Fort Nelson: Gerri F. Young, 1980.

Films

African American Trailblazers - Building the Alaska Highway. National Park Service, US Department of the Interior. 5 min. Undated but footage is from 1942-43. https://www.youtube.com/watch?v=ejQ-QF2SvKM

Building The Alaskan Highway, National Geographic Magazine. 45 min. https://www.youtube.com/watch?v=3sDHe2qHHw44

Fractured Land, dir. Damien Gillis and Fiona Rayher. Two Island Films, 2015. Voted a "Top 10 audience favourite" at HotDocs Festival in Toronto. About George Behn's grandson, the activist and lawyer Caleb Behn.

Pincers on Japan, dir. James Beverage, narrated by Lorne Greene. NFB, 19 min. 1943. http://onf-nfb.gc.ca/en/our-collection/?idfilm=17275

Walking Through Memory Lane with our North Peace Elders: Treasured Chronicles II. Anne Callison video, April 3, 2007. Fort St. John: Hill Computing, 2007.

Websites (these links will change but may help readers to search)

Alberta Geneological Society, Northwestern Alberta Obituary Index. http://www.abgenealogy.ca/gp-obituary-database

BC Ministry of Transportation and Infrastructure. https://www.tranbc.ca/2017/08/10/why-building-of-the-alaska-highway-is-still-an-epic-feat-75-years-later/

Blueberry River Indian Band *v.* Canada, 1995. http://www.indigenousbar.ca/cases/apsassin.htm

CODE Canada. www.code.ngo

Doig River First Nation. *Dane Wajich: Dana-zaa Stories & Songs: Dreamers and the Land:* http://www.virtualmuseum.ca/sgc-cms/expositions-exhibitions/danewajich/

Local History Book Index of Indexes. http://users.rootsweb.com/

Larry Evans. "Looking Back: Rural Communities North of Fort St. John." http://www.alaskahighwaynews.ca/opinion/columnists/looking-back-rural-communities-north-of-fort-st-john-1.1146186. June 17, 2010.

Fort Nelson Public Library Northern Rockies Regional Municipality Archives. https://ehive.com/collections/6505/fort-nelson-public-library-nrrm-archives

Fort Nelson Heritage Museum. http://www.fortnelsonmuseum.ca/

Fort St. John Tourism. http://tourismfortstjohn.ca/what-to-do/history-heritage/history-of-the-area

Fort St. John North Peace Museum. http://www.fsjmuseum.com

Paul Haavardsrud. "The lowdown on the Montney. Canada's next big energy bet has the same high stakes as oilsands." CBC online, November 2, 2016. http://www.cbc.ca/news/business/montney-natural-gas-challenges-1.3829007

Joint report of the National Energy Board, BC Oil and Gas Commission and the Alberta Energy Regulator, 2013. https://www.neb-one.gc.ca/nrg/sttstc/ntrlgs/rprt/ltmtptntlmntnyfrmtn2013/ltmtptntlmntnyfrmtn2013fq-eng.html

Bruce Holland. "Ghost Lodges on the Alaska Highway." August 4, 2016. www.ourhomehas6wheels.com/ghost-lodges-onthe-alaska-highway/

Military Communications and Electronics Museum, Kingston, ON. https://www.candemuseum.org/exhibits

Open Letter on the Health Impacts of the Site C Dam, December 4, 2017, by the BC members of the Canadian Association of Physicians for the Environment. https://bccapevolunteers.wordpress.com/2017/12/04/open-letter-on-the-health-impacts-of-the-site-c-dam/

Our Alaska Highway. http://ouralaskahighway.com/?page_id=1011

Saskatoon Mountain Natural Area. https://www.albertaparks.ca/parks/northwest/saskatoon-mountain-na/

Słownik geograficzny Królestwa Polskiego i innych krajów słowiańskich. http://dir.icm.edu.pl/pl/Slownik_geograficzny/Tom_I

South Peace Historical Society. http://calverley.ca

Jonny Wakefield. "For Kwadacha First Nation, healing from W.A.C. Bennett Dam a work in progress." Dawson Creek Mirror, June 13, 2016. http://www.dawsoncreekmirror.ca/regional-news/site-c/for-kwadacha-first-nation-healing-from-w-a-c-bennett-dam-a-work-in-progress-1.2277453

Yad Veshem, Holocaust Remembrance Center. http://www.yadvashem.org

Yahad In-Unum. http://www.yahadinunum.org

Yukon Archives: The Alaska Highway: A Yukon Perspective. www.alaskahighwayarchives.ca/en/resources/credits.php

Photo Credits (and Vignettes, where further credit is needed or helpful)

page 1 (left), 18, 23-26, 114, 138 (bottom), 158, 175, 176: Erín Moure.

page 1 (centre & right), 3, 51, 55, 56, 58-66, 80, 85-88, 94, 101, 103, 104, 106-109, 112, 118, 125, 126, 134, 135, 147, 151, 155, 161, 163, 166, 168, 170, 172 (left): Anne Callison.

page 5: from a newspaper clipping in Anne Callison's archives, not identified.

page 12: map from Alaska Highway tourist pamphlet, ~1945 (public domain).

page 21, 111: internet (not credited, public domain)

Vignette p. 35: *Gat Tah Kwą, Chief Montney, and the Dane-ẕaa People*, reprinted with permission of the Doig River First Nation (via Councillor Attachie) from www.virtualmuseum.ca/sgc-cms/expositions-exhibitions/danewajich/english/places/montney.php.

page 40, 41, 44, 50, 52, 76, 98, 105 and Vignette p. 75: from *Mountain Trails*, by Daisy Callison, reprinted with permission of the estate of Daisy Callison.

page 48: newspaper cutting in Anne Callison archive (not credited).

page 70: C-and-E-museum.org, exhibit taken down. Manual quoted is in public domain.

page 73: US Office of War Information. Overseas Picture Division. Washington Division, ©1944. In public domain.

page 74: Courtesy of the Fort St. John North Peace Museum. #2011.39.34.

Vignette p. 89-90: "Lodema George: Fort Nelson's First Lady," compiled from newspaper articles online in Fort Nelson archives, from information in *The Fort Nelson Story*, from other references on the internet, and from personal memory.

page 119: "Ghost Lodges of the Alaska Highway." Image in public domain.

Vignette p. 120: "Not Just on the Ground but in the Air," compiled from online information at Virtualmuseum.ca and corrected by Pat's granddaughter Sandy Baker with help from her mom Joan, Pat's daughter.

page 137, 138 (top), 157: Bill Moure Jr.

page 140, 141, 142: maps from *Atlas of land cover, industrial land uses and industrial-caused land changes in the Peace Region of British Columbia* ISBN: 978-0-9780976-4-6. Edmonton: Global Forest Watch Canada, 2012. (Global Forest Watch Canada closed in 2017; its reports were to be uploaded to databasin.org for public use; maps are used here under principles of non-profit sharing).

Vignette p. 148-149: *"Just a minute!"* drawn from publicly available material; read to George Behn by Sally Behn, Fort Nelson First Nation, corrected for accuracy, and published with their approval.

Vignette p. 156: "Fishing with John Callison, by Bill Moure" is drawn from an private email sent me by Bill and is published with approval.

page 172 (right): Sandy Baker.

page 182: One copy is in Collections Canada, Accession Number 78903/45. Map is in public domain.

"Territories ceded under Treaty No. 8 and the Indian tribes therein." (Department of Indian Affairs, Canada, 1900).

[Note: In this book, names of Indigenous nations in the NE of today's BC are spelled as they are on the map at tribalnationsmaps.com, 2017. Old colonial names were Slavey or Slave (for Dene Tha'), South Slavey (for Acho Dene koe), Sekani (for Tsek'ene) and Beaver (for Dane-zaa). Resources from 2009 at UBC's Xwi7xwa Library at xwi7xwa.library.ubc.ca/collections/indigenous-knowledge-organization/ use the names Slave, Sekani, and Dunne-za.]

Appendix A: Velyki Hlibovychi in the 20ᵗʰ Century
Великі Глібовичі

Velyki Hlibovychi (Greater Hlibovychi, with "hlib" meaning "bread"), the village of the Grendys and Hamulyaks, was one of the huge Polish-Lithuanian aristocratic estates that had existed since 1500. In 1880, the village had 1,637 residents: 1452 Greek Catholic (Ukrainian), 158 Roman Catholic (Poles), and 27 Jewish. There was a primary school, a credit union, a metal smelting company. By 1930, there were 2785 residents. There was the Stefcha bank, the Kolko Rolnicze cooperative, brickworks (owner Y. Zyukh), mills (owners J. Shidlovsky and Count Alfred Potocki), along with several pubs (owners H. Aker, N. Alter, J. Millet, A. and J. Ziukha), carpenter shops (P. Basht and V. Damka), a blacksmith (M. Buczkowski), and tailors (F. Philas and J. Welsh). The village grew to 3,280 by 1939: 1980 Ukrainians, 600 Poles, 600 Latynnyky, 100 Jews.

The First World War saw armies of both sides—Austro-Hungarian and Russian—in the village, with fierce fighting at the front further east, at the bustling market town of Bibrka. Dead soldiers reeked in the fields for days. After the armistice in Western Europe in 1918, Eastern Europe was still at war, as Ukrainian nationalists fought for the independence of Ukraine and against inclusion in Poland. Some from Hlibovichi served in the Ukrainian Galician Army.

In 1921, the area was joined to Poland, which began repressions against the Ukrainian population. Still, the Grendys family returned from the USA, hoping for peace. The village was close to the modern town of Bibrka, where the Thursday farmers' market was held. Nelly Grendys was known to say that because they came from a mixed village, her family could shop at all the stands: Ukrainian, Polish, Jewish, and German! They were on good terms with all and proud of their culture.

In July, 1930, after Tom and Nelly Grendys emigrated a second time (with Tom sure a war was brewing), the Ukrainian nationalist underground army robbed a Post Office money transport from the Hlibovychi railway station to the county office in Bibrka, six kilometres away, killing the Polish police escort. Polish reprisals were harsh—the boy scout organization Plast was shut down, and its leaders arrested, accused of training militants. Several neighbours were imprisoned.

In September 1939, Soviet authorities arrived and the area was joined to Soviet Ukraine. There were arrests and deportations to Siberia of anyone considered to be "hostile elements." People of mixed villages by and large were considered "unreliable." When the USSR evicted families of Polish colonists (sent by Poland after World War One) and foresters (traditionally a Polish job on the estates) in the Lviv region on January 21, 1940, four families were removed from the village. Soviet power lasted but a short time. In June 1941, German troops took over Galicia.

> And so… we were children, all barefoot, you know… So we dash out of the house to watch. On this road from Vybranivka, there were two men riding on motorcycles, Germans. With the cross [swastika], and all that. Our women… were thinking that Germans "will bring Ukraine" [i.e. make Ukraine independent]. So they came out on the street with flowers, greeting them. One guy who was in Germany before the war came out of his house and greets them in German. So yes, I remember the Germans. But what they did later [what atrocities they committed], oh dear Lord, dear Lord, dear Lord. —*Maria Zadorozhnaya, born 1927*

Nazi occupation saw creation of a regional ghetto in Bibrka, where Jews from the region and from Poland were held. As their village lay along the railway, residents of Velyki Hlibovychi saw the passage northward only of sealed Nazi trains. They may not have known that the trains ended at the Belzec extermination camp, but they knew people never came back. Over a thousand Jews from the Bibrka ghetto were force-marched through the village in 1942 and onto the trains. Thousands more were murdered later in 1942 and 1943 nearby, most at the Bibrka sandpit. Locals were requisitioned to assist the killers in tasks like digging, guarding, and removing furniture from now-empty houses. "Blood flowed out of the soil onto the road for days." Neighbours wrote the Grendys family in Alberta with news of these crimes; the letters, which my mother told me of, have not survived.

Nazi rule lasted until July 1944, when Soviet troops again arrived. Deportations and repressions began once more. Those identified as "Poles" were sent west to Poland. They split families to make it difficult for people to return. A whole street of Storonka, on the far side of the river, suffered this fate. Stalin sent Ukrainians deported from the Polish side to live in the homes. 139 villagers were forced into the Red Army and sent to the front. In mass arrests from September 23 to October 3, 1944, 120 villagers vanished. Many were deported to Siberia, including Grendys relatives, not to return until the 1960s, broken in health, and unwilling to speak of their tribulations.

In the late 1980s, the prospect of Ukraine's independence became real. After the proclamation of independence, a monument to the "Fighters for the freedom of Ukraine" was created and crosses placed where nationalist fighters had died in the village. There is a stone memorial too to the freeing of the serfs in the 18th century. There is yet no monument to the memory of their murdered Jewish neighbours.

For a couple hundred years, there had also been an ethnic German colony west of Bibkra, called Ernsdorf. After its residents fled at war's end with the Nazis (as collaborators, they wouldn't have been spared by the Soviets), the colony's buildings became a collective tractor station, and then, after independence, a truck depot.

The village of Velyki Hlibovychi is a quiet place today. Its population is about 2000, half of what it was before the Second World War. The last time I was there in 2011, there were two tiny grocery stores, one closed pyrogy house, and one small bar. Bibrka, still the region's main town, has never regained its prosperity. People now go to shop in Lviv, a short distance north along a modern highway.

The Greek Catholic Church from 1930 was restored in 2008. In 2011, there was a field of weeds where the old wooden Roman Catholic church stood (another is a relic on a hill); the Polish school is a private home. The Ukrainian elementary school down the road is active. Students in higher grades are bussed to Bibrka, where there is a Roman Catholic Church and a Russian Orthodox Church. The remains of the synagogue in Bibrka are in private hands, and wind and snow enter there. Unlike in other villages where people have worked to protect Jewish graves and sites of worship as sacred to memory, in Bibrka the old synagogue is almost completely fallen down.

I am the only family member from Canada to have visited Velyki Hlibovychi, birthplace of Anna and Marja Grendysz, and of their parents. I also went to Bibrka, to honour the memory of the Messers. Their family's absence, in particular, instructs me as to why my grandpa longed to find a life without war. I have the gaze of Isak Messer to thank for the amazing photo (page 26) he took of my emigrating family, in which Anne's wee sister—who grew up to be my mother—struggles out of her father's arms.

www.ingramcontent.com/pod-product-compliance
Lightning Source LLC
LaVergne TN
LVHW011350080426
835511LV00005B/225